747518

D1278557

BF   Albin, Rochelle
561   Semmel, 1945-
.A46
1983   Emotions

DATE			

THE CHICAGO PUBLIC LIBRARY
EDUCATION & PHILOSOPHY

Social Sciences and History Division

© THE BAKER & TAYLOR CO.

Emotions

CHOICES

GUIDES FOR TODAY'S WOMAN

Emotions

Rochelle Semmel Albin

The Westminster Press
Philadelphia

Copyright © 1983 Rochelle Semmel Albin

All rights reserved—no part of this book may be reproduced in any form without permission in writing from the publisher, except by a reviewer who wishes to quote brief passages in connection with a review in magazine or newspaper.

Book Design by Alice Derr

First edition

Published by The Westminster Press®
Philadelphia, Pennsylvania

PRINTED IN THE UNITED STATES OF AMERICA
9 8 7 6 5 4 3 2 1

BF
561
.A46
1983

To Jean Baker Miller

Library of Congress Cataloging in Publication Data

Albin, Rochelle Semmel, 1945–
   Emotions.

   (Choices : guides for today's woman)
   Bibliography: p.
   1. Emotions. 2.Women—Psychology. I. Title.
II. Series: Choices.
BF561.A46 1983   152.4′024042   83-10187
ISBN 0-664-24540-4 (pbk.)

CONTENTS

PUBLISHER'S ACKNOWLEDGMENT

The publisher gratefully acknowledges the advice of several distinguished scholars in planning this series. Virginia Mollenkott, Arlene Swidler, Phyllis Trible, and Ann Ulanov helped shape the goals of the series, identify vital topics, and locate knowledgeable authors. Views expressed in the books, of course, are those of the individual writers and not of the advisers.

ACKNOWLEDGMENTS

Discussions with four clinical psychologists at various stages of the manuscript clarified both ideas and text. Dr. Nancy Lundy helped generously during the book's preliminary stages. Dr. Edwin Ellis and Dr. Judy Jordan commented perceptively on an early draft. Dr. Adele Kauffman was an insightful listener, always willing to talk through concepts and their description. The book is much better as a result of their contributions.

Friends, and my brother and his family, also contributed in a special way. I thank them for their support.

PREFACE

We live in a society that has a long tradition of valuing the rational and intellectual aspects of our lives over the emotional. Not only is thinking considered more valuable and more important than feeling, but it is viewed as more controllable and thus less dangerous. We have come to believe that we can control our thoughts better than we can control our emotions, and that, because of this, emotions represent the weaker side of human nature.

This tradition puts women in a bind. While men have always been considered rational—and therefore in tune with what our society values most—women have been considered emotional. Women do seem to be more in touch than men with certain important human feelings, such as those caused by sadness, weakness, passivity, helplessness, and the need to be connected to other people.

Women's greater capacity to experience such emotions is actually a strength rather than a liability, as we have assumed it was for so long. And men, by viewing these emotions as signs of weakness, miss out on a whole side of human experience and a way of connecting themselves to others.

Human emotional life is incredibly rich and varied. Its complexity can provide great pleasure, but it can also seriously disrupt our everyday lives and relationships. Emotions rarely work perfectly or smoothly, and sometimes we cannot stay on an even keel—for instance, when a stressful event such as a divorce or a death occurs. But even pleasant situations, like a wedding or the birth of a child, may temporarily throw our emotions out of kilter.

By clarifying what emotions are, where they might come from, and how they affect us and others, this book attempts to help women to understand their feelings and handle them more comfortably and more constructively. There are no easy answers, but there are ways of coping that can make our emotional lives richer, more pleasurable, and less troublesome.

R. S. A.

Cambridge, Massachusetts

CHAPTER 1

What Is an Emotion?

AN EMOTION IS A FEELING INSIDE US

We usually think of emotions as specific feelings such as love, anger, and joy. Those are the labels we have learned to give the various feelings that come from inside us. The label we give to a specific feeling determines how we think about that feeling and how we act. For instance, a woman who feels anger acts differently from a woman who feels joy. Much depends on how we identify what we feel.

We begin to distinguish one emotion from another as very young children, as our parents respond differently to our varying feelings and behavior. As infants, we experienced feelings that were either good (such as those experienced when our mothers held us or fed us) or bad (such as hunger). The capacity to distinguish all kinds of things from one another—what is ours from what belongs to playmates, people's voices and faces, the seasons of the year—increases gradually as we grow from infants to children to adults. This capacity to see more and more differences in what we experience continues throughout our lives, and we become better at distinguishing among our own feelings and those of others. Psychologists

consider this process a crucial aspect of human development.

We can observe these changes in our own children
who may confuse anger with hatred, for instance. They
know that they are feeling something unpleasant, that
they feel hurt and wounded by another person, and that
they feel something bad toward that person. But they
have not yet learned that anger may be transient and hate
longer-lasting, nor have they yet learned to tell the
difference between the two feelings.

Teenagers are often uncertain and confused about
what love is and whether what they are feeling is the
"real thing." But by our twenties and thirties we are
usually more able to tell the difference between liking
another person, feeling infatuated romantically, and feeling real love, which involves commitment and caring.

As we get better at telling one emotion from another
and labeling what we feel more accurately, we also begin
to think about our feelings. We no longer simply feel
angry or sad—we start to wonder why we feel that way
and what to do about it. We are no longer a bundle of
good and bad feelings, like the infant. Our feelings have
names and causes, and sometimes even actions, associat-
ed with them.

The capacity to think about our emotions also improves our ability to control them. We still feel them, but
we develop some choices about what to do with them.
We understand better what has caused a particular feeling, and we can decide whether we want to keep the
feeling inside us, express it in some way (such as crying
or withdrawing for a while to be alone with it), or act on it
in a way that usually affects other people.

These differences in how we handle our feelings can
be seen from watching young children who have just
begun to play with others their age. When they feel

envious of a toy that belongs to a playmate, they may simply take it. When they feel angry at losing a game, they may scream or cry. Children usually express their feelings spontaneously, and often act on what they feel. But an adult who envies her neighbor's garden does not steal the flowers or spoil them. She has many more choices about what to do with her envy than the child has. She can accept her feelings and live with them. She can learn to enjoy the beauty of the garden. She can tell her neighbor how stunning the garden is and how she wishes she had one of her own. She can start a garden herself to wash away the envy she feels toward her neighbor. She can allow her anger to build, and become more jealous and resentful. She can even use physical exercise—running or swimming, perhaps—to ease her unpleasant feelings.

We do not live in a vacuum, isolated from other people, and our emotions do not occur in isolation from human relationships. The capacity to distinguish our emotions not only develops with age, but the emotions of those around us also affect the labels we give to what we ourselves feel. Psychologists have found that emotions are contagious, and that if we are not exactly sure what we are feeling or what might be the "right" feeling in a particular situation, we depend on the actions of others to name our own emotions and to guide our own behavior.

Five-year-old Gloria, for example, expected that her first visit for a haircut would be frightening, because her mother had described that she would "have less hair" and that the hair would be clipped away and fall to the floor. But when Gloria arrived for her haircut (the hairdresser was a woman who cut the hair of children very frequently), she found other children there playing and laughing. They giggled over how funny it was to watch the hair fall to the floor and how special and pretty each girl looked once it was over. The feelings of these children had such an effect on Gloria that her fright turned to excitement and she began to wait eagerly for her turn in the chair.

Similar situations occur when we are grown up. In fact, there are certain periods in our lives when we depend heavily on others for signs about how we are supposed to feel, how we are supposed to express those feelings, and how we are supposed to act on them. For instance, teenagers watch carefully how their age-mates feel and behave in varying situations. Afraid of looking too different or standing out from their friends, they may "catch" emotions more easily than either children or adults.

But even adults sometimes look toward others for cues about what they should be feeling and how to express those feelings or act on them. Harriet, for instance, had conflicting feelings about her father's remarriage just one year after her mother died. She felt happy that her father, who had been extremely lonely and isolated for months after his wife's death, had found a new partner whom he loved and who seemed to make a good companion for him. But Harriet had been close to her mother and still missed her very much, so she had trouble understanding how her father, who had been happily married, could take another mate so quickly. She also felt angry. Harriet at times expressed her mixed feelings by crying, but she had no idea how to behave at her father's upcoming wedding.

With the wedding approaching, Harriet found it difficult to be with her father and his wife-to-be. Not knowing how to act, she began to watch the reaction of her two sisters when they were all together, and even started to talk privately with them about their feelings. They had not been as close to their mother as Harriet had been, so they found it easier to feel happy about their father's new life. As Harriet saw how comfortable her sisters felt around the new couple, she began to feel better about the marriage and more able to feel happy for her father.

Even though as we grow up, we become more able to name and distinguish our feelings and to decide whether and how to act on them, the process is never perfect. We can never completely control our emotions. As adults, we can still become confused at times about what we are feeling and unsure about how to express feelings and how to act on them.

Because human beings are capable of experiencing so many emotions, knowing exactly what we are feeling is sometimes difficult. We may also find it hard to figure out if we want to act on those feelings, and how. At times, we may express feelings (by crying, for instance) or act on feelings (by impulsively quitting a job) even though we would rather keep things to ourselves. We may feel especially confused during those times when many different things are happening at once and we cannot easily sort out the causes of certain feelings.

Martha had exactly this problem when she finished graduate school and separated from her husband just one year after moving to a new city. She was able to find only a part-time job, and that proved difficult, because the work was new and she worried a lot about succeeding at it. Because she worked only two days a week, Martha was dependent on her husband for rent and living expenses, and she had plenty of idle time to dwell on her situation.

Martha felt alternately angry, depressed, and anxious, but it was hard for her to sort out exactly what was causing each feeling. Was she depressed over her husband, or over her inability to find a full-time job? Was she angry that she could not support herself, or that she could not live as comfortably as when she and her husband were together? Martha found herself uncertain about what she was feeling and why.

Feelings can take us by surprise. We may visit a place we have never been before—a new church or a new family—and suddenly feel angry, sad, or anxious without any idea why. It is difficult to figure out what is causing the unexpected emotions. We may never fully understand our surprising reaction. But we can observe the people and places that stirred up these feelings and accept our feelings. By doing this, we get to know ourselves a bit better.

Even though we are more able to distinguish, name, and handle our emotions as we grow older, it is not a simple task and is often complicated by difficult situations in our lives. We may find ourselves confused about what we are feeling or why we are feeling a particular way. We have the potential for rich and varied feelings, but we do not have a foolproof way of living with our emotions.

DO EMOTIONS MAKE US ACT?

Emotions such as love, anger, and hate are feelings that come from inside us, usually in response to things that happen in our lives. When Jill's older sister had her first baby, both Jill and her parents felt overjoyed. When Charlene's teenage daughter qualified for the Junior Olympics in swimming, the whole family felt proud and happy. When Dan, much-loved ninety-year-old grandfather of fifteen children, died, they all felt very sad and grieved for many months because they missed him so much.

Emotions can stimulate new thoughts, new imagination, and new action. Jill's joy at becoming an aunt sent her running to the hospital every chance she had, and then to her sister's house as often as possible. She helped to take care of the baby and experienced, together with her sister, the joy of the infant's presence. Charlene's family acted on their feelings of pride and joy too. They invited Charlene and her teammates, who had also qualified for the Olympics, to a party and celebrated grandly the youngsters' success. They all looked forward to accompanying her to Florida, where the Junior Olympics would take place. Charlene herself began to be excited about possibly making the regular Olympics in Europe the following year. And Dan's children and grandchildren, after mourning his death for almost a year, decided they wanted to do something special to remember his warmth and love for them. They donated a piece of the land around his house to the city for a playground for young children.

Sometimes it is fairly easy to see the connection between what we feel and how we behave. This connection was pretty clear to Jill, to Charlene, and to Dan's children and grandchildren. At other times, the link between how we feel and how we act can be less clear— for instance, when we have two or more feelings that conflict, or when we feel overwhelmed by our emotions and cannot easily sort them out, or when we are unsure about what a particular event and our emotional reaction to it means to us.

The meaning we give to our emotions helps us figure out how to act when we feel a certain way. We know that all people do not express themselves the same way or act alike when they feel sad or angry or joyful. These differences come partly from the different meanings individuals give to their feelings. For some of us, feelings are very intense, whereas others experience milder emotions.

Janet thought that feelings of guilt were bad and meant that she did not care enough about the people around her. She did not dare express her guilt, because she feared that her husband and children would find out that she did not care about them. Margaret, on the other hand, believed that to feel guilty meant that another person had asked for something that she could not give and that these feelings were not bad at all but were a sign that she and her friend had to talk over what had happened between them. To Janet, feeling guilty meant not caring for other people and led her to hold her guilt inside. To Margaret, feeling guilty meant that something had gone wrong in a relationship and called for some honest talking with her friend.

Emotions themselves—love, hate, joy, and anger—do not make us act in certain ways. Rather, it is the meaning we give to our emotions that may lead to certain behavior. For many of us, the difficult part of dealing with our feelings only begins with learning to distinguish among them and learning to name them. Figuring out what they mean to us continues throughout our lives and at times requires hard work. Often we are unaware that in between our feelings and our actions comes some serious thinking about what those feelings mean. When a feeling is particularly intense, it becomes even more difficult to decide whether to express it or act on it and how. In these situations, we lose some of our capacity for choice.

Jane, a single woman at age twenty-eight, had been feeling more and more envious of her friends' lives. They all seemed richer, happier, and more settled than she, with their husbands and families and homes in the suburbs. Over the last couple of years, her envy became more intense and she began to feel deeply jealous of their lives, even though she had many joys and successes of a different sort in her own life. Envy and jealousy eventually turned to anger, and it became more painful for her to see the friends she had grown up with and known for years.

When Jane became unable to enjoy her own work as a teacher, which she had always loved and been very good at, she started to wonder what had gone wrong. What did it mean that after all these years of friendship she could no longer bear to see her friends, and that after all those years of work she could barely make it to school each morning?

Once before, after the death of Jane's grandmother, to whom she had been very attached, Jane had sought out her minister and talked with him several times about her love for her grandmother and how much she missed her. The minister, who had known the older woman, grieved together with Jane and helped her accept her grandmother's death.

Now, once again overwhelmed by her feelings and not knowing what to do to make her life more comfortable, Jane went to her minister. Although it was difficult to tell him how envious, jealous, and angry she had become, and how unsatisfying her work was, she hoped he could shed light on what all the feelings meant and what she could do about them.

After talking with her for a few months, her minister, a trained counselor, helped Jane realize how neglected she felt. All her friends seemed to be taken care of by their husbands, whom they took care of in turn. But for Jane, everything in her life was her responsibility, and neither burdens nor pleasures were shared regularly with another person.

Jane also began to understand that although she had never felt she wanted children of her own, believing that teaching fulfilled well her enjoyment of youngsters, growing older may have changed things for her. Her friends' marriages and children looked satisfying and comfortable. Jane began to understand the meaning of the envy, jealousy, anger, and dissatisfaction she had endured during the past couple of years. Now that she had been helped to understand the meaning of her feelings, she could begin to figure out what to do about them and how to act on them.

Once we realize the importance of the meaning we give to our emotions, we have many more choices about how to handle them and what to do with them. We are no longer stuck just feeling and maybe acting, or feeling and keeping those feelings inside.

One source of conflict between people who are close to each other is the differing meanings they may give to the same emotion. Whether we consider an emotion "good" or "bad" affects whether we express it or act on it. George, for instance, thought anger toward another person was to be expressed and told his wife so when she angered him, sometimes even yelling at her. Megan, on the other hand, thought she was supposed to keep angry feelings inside because they were "bad." Not only did George's behavior shock and upset her but it made her angrier still and she could express none of it. It took some serious talk between George and Megan for them to understand the meanings they gave to their angry feelings and to accommodate to each other's individual style.

But it was hard for them to change. While they understood each other better, George and Megan still usually expressed their anger very differently. In fact, George started playing tennis several times a week to express some of his pent-up anger by hitting a ball instead of yelling at Megan.

NOT THE MIND ALONE: THE ROLE OF OUR BODY IN FEELINGS

We each have a mind and a body that work together to give us a rich emotional life. Our minds and bodies are not separate entities that have little to do with each other but rather are always interacting to produce a variety of feelings, thoughts, and actions. We can understand, then, that our varying emotions do not occur simply because we label them in different ways, as we have learned to do, but also because our nervous systems are set up to react biochemically in certain situations.

Some of us who have been in very frightening situations may have noticed, for instance, that our hearts beat faster, that we breathe faster, and that we have more energy. This may happen in response to something that threatens us from the outside (a bear at our campsite, perhaps) or when we feel threatened by feelings from the inside (anger that may get out of control, for example). It is these kinds of physiological changes that we call emotions.

You are comfortably dozing in bed on a Sunday morning when the doorbell rings at 8 A.M. and immediately stirs up fear that something is wrong. Your thoughts wander anxiously from one possibility to the next. Is it the police coming to tell you about an auto accident in your family? Is it a telegram with bad news about your sick mother who lives in Canada? You feel your heart beat faster, you start perspiring, you develop goose pimples—you have automatically labeled the unexpected intrusion as dangerous in some way. You make your way downstairs, open the door, and find a florist delivering roses for your thirtieth birthday. You smile, your symptoms disappear, and you think how kind your friend is. Your mood changes from fear to joy.

The physical feelings you experienced came from the action of hormones on the transmission of nerve impulses in the brain. When the doorbell rang, your brain signaled your adrenal gland to produce more adrenalin, which increased your heart rate, your respiratory rate, and your energy level. The excess adrenalin prepared you to act on your fear, to feel frightened and run downstairs. For many of us, it is the *feeling* of our heart and lungs working faster that we call anxiety or fear.

Scientists have recently discovered that emotions such as joy may also be related to changes in brain biochemistry. The brain seems to have quantities of a natural drug—endorphins—that produces joy. People who run many miles at a time often report that they feel euphoric and joyful afterward, and researchers now think that the exercise produces an excess of endorphins in the brain which, in turn, produces the pleasant emotions.

Scientists have also found chemicals in the brain that may make people feel depressed. Preliminary research has found that very depressed people may lack enough endorphins to feel good. It is also possible that they may lack certain chemicals that transmit messages between nerves, messages that cause the rest of us to eat when hungry, sleep when tired, and feel energetic during the day.

While a biochemical reaction may "cause" a certain emotion, the opposite may be true too. Sometimes we feel angry or anxious just thinking about things in our lives. Weeks before an exam, or months before our wedding, we may begin to worry about the test questions, about failing, or whether we are making the right choice of a mate. These thoughts may actually change our brain biochemistry, so that we begin to feel anxious far in advance of the actual event.

Scientists are still trying to figure out how the body and the mind interact to produce emotions. The most important discovery so far is that it is not only the mind, but also the biochemistry of our bodies, particularly our brains, that makes our feelings.

EMOTIONS FEEL GOOD AND BAD

Some emotions are more difficult to endure than others. Some feel good and some feel bad. People also differ in the intensity of an emotion that they can tolerate. We all know people who reach the "boiling point" faster than others and start letting everyone know how angry they are soon after they begin to feel that way. Women tend to hold their anger in and not express it as much as men. Their "boiling points" are thus much higher.

Anger is one emotion that seems to be uncomfortable for everyone, partly because it feels unpleasant but also because we fear the impact our anger might have on others. Because of these fears, many women choose to keep their anger inside and hide it, but this often makes them even more uncomfortable, for they must continue to struggle to keep the feeling to themselves.

Some feelings are so intense that they demand expression, but we may be too frightened of them to let them out. When this happens, we may express them indirectly or transfer them to others. We may feel furious at our boss for not recognizing our work, but unable to let him know how we feel because we fear losing our job or losing control when we begin to talk to him. Instead, we come home and yell at a roommate for not making her bed, something we would ordinarily not even notice.

Hate is another unpleasant feeling, one that may affect our entire emotional life. Feeling hate toward one or more persons over a long period of time can crowd out good feelings such as love and joy. Anger, hate, and bitterness may be all that is left, giving us an emotional life that is more painful than pleasurable.

But even pleasurable emotions are sometimes difficult to endure. For instance, love can be very hard and troubling during long periods in a relationship. Love is difficult not only for adults but also for young children, who may feel hatred toward their parents, whom they need desperately and whom they love. Because children are so dependent on their parents for their survival, love mixed with hate can be quite frightening for them. Parents who have accepted the imperfections and inconsistencies in their own feelings will be more able to help children accept theirs too.

Love in a marriage is also at times difficult to endure. Abby loved her husband deeply, and for fourteen years they and their two children lived peacefully and happily. But changes at Peter's job began to upset the balance they had nurtured during those years. The managerial structure of the company for which Peter worked was reorganized and resulted in a situation that made him very unhappy. Peter constantly sought opinions from his wife about how he should respond. When she offered her ideas, he ridiculed them and insisted, "You just don't understand how things are for me there."

Making matters worse, Abby began to sense that Peter was getting himself deeper and deeper in trouble at work arguing over the changes that his co-workers had begun to accept. She disagreed with his attitude and worried about whether he would be able to stay at the job. She found it difficult to be nurturant and supportive, as she had been through all their years of marriage, and felt guilty about her "failure." She began to see more and more imperfections in her husband. Not until Peter sat down with his boss to talk things out did their marriage begin to settle down and the expression of love become easier. But for months afterward, Peter and Abby still found it hard to talk calmly about things.

Some emotions are unpleasant and difficult, but they can be useful warning signs that something is wrong. Edna felt blue and depressed after the birth of her first baby. She and her husband had been happily married for three years before Matthew came along, and neither could understand why Edna did not feel happier after the birth of their much-wanted child.

Edna's depression was particularly puzzling because it occurred at a time in her life when she was supposed to be happy. She felt angry and cheated that she could not enjoy the first weeks and months of her baby's life. A fight with her husband one night when he arrived home from the office late lasted for several days, during which Edna realized the meaning behind her blues. From the time they had gotten married, she and her husband had shared everything, but now, with the birth of Matthew, things changed radically. Her husband was at work all day, and she was at home with the baby. One of the most important events in their marriage, taking care of their first baby, had been left to her alone and went unshared by her husband.

Edna's depression had been a sign that something was wrong. When she finally thought she had figured out what the problem might be, she and Peter tried to make some decisions about how to deal with it and how to share raising Matthew. Things never worked out just as Edna would have liked, because Peter had a lot of trouble assuming responsibility for the care of his infant son. But at least they could talk about it, and that helped Edna.

Few emotions feel purely good or bad. Even hate, which usually feels unpleasant, may feel good at times when we feel maliciously wounded by another person. Whether an emotion feels pleasurable or unpleasurable depends on what it means to us, on how we express it and act on it, and on the situation in which it occurs. In some situations, the same emotion may be more difficult to endure than in other situations. Feeling anger toward someone who acted rudely toward us may be more bearable than feeling anger toward an elderly parent.

Emotions are more difficult to endure when we are ambivalent or conflicted about them and when we are unsure whether we are even entitled to feel them. At age ninety-two, Gina's father, who lived with Gina and her husband, remained physically active and sociable. But he had a habit of putting away things that belonged to his daughter and forgetting where they were. Gina realized her father was older and not as sharp as he used to be, but she also felt angry when she needed something and could not find it. She felt guilty for yelling at him when she was rushing off to work late, after hunting for the briefcase he had put away in the coat closet or the scarf he had hung with the dishtowels. Gina was not sure she was entitled to feel angry at her elderly father when he did things he probably could not help, and her love for him made her feelings of anger even more painful.

Human beings enjoy rich emotional lives that are complex rather than simple. Even the emotions that our culture tells us should always be wonderful—love, for example—have their painful sides. Nevertheless, emotions such as love and joy are meant to provide more pleasure to ourselves and to others than emotions such as jealousy and hate, which can be painful to tolerate and hurtful to those around us.

WE DO NOT ALWAYS CHOOSE OUR EMOTIONS

We have many varied emotions that enrich our lives, but we do not have control over what we might feel at different times. We may want to love someone but, no matter how hard we try, feel only indifference. We may want to feel joy at a friend's success, but feel only envy instead. We may want to feel anger at people who have hurt us, but instead feel sorry for them because they do not know how to be kind to others.

As we grow older, we learn more about which people and which situations evoke good and bad feelings. We learn to stay away from people who hurt us or make us angry, and from situations that we fear or that make us sad. We may refuse to drive through the poor parts of town because we feel sad about the people who do not have adequate homes and clothing. And we may learn to stay away from the woman who used to be our friend but whose constant jealousy made us feel guilty over our own good fortune.

As we get to know ourselves better and know more about how we respond and what we like, we become more able to seek out people and situations that make us feel happy and comfortable. Nevertheless, we lack total control over events and situations and often find ourselves—at work, for instance—with people who make us feel angry or guilty, or at parties with people more glamorous than ourselves who make us feel poor and dowdy. We cannot always choose our emotions, but we have more choices when it comes to expressing them and acting on them. We sometimes can choose what to do with them.

The range of possibilities for dealing with our emotions increases as we grow older. As we grow up, we learn, by watching others and through trial and error, which methods might be more effective for handling our anxiety, our joy, and our shame. We learn not only those methods that make us more comfortable but also the impact of our choices on others. We may be most comfortable hiding in our room as soon as we get anxious, but those around us may feel more comfortable if we first talk about our shaking knees and sick stomach rather than withdrawing and leaving others to figure out what is wrong.

EMOTIONS MAY BE USED CONSTRUCTIVELY OR DESTRUCTIVELY

There are both constructive and destructive ways to handle our emotions. Our feelings have the potential for hurting others, but they can also harm *us* and do damage to relationships we value. They also have the potential, if used constructively, to improve our relations with others and to help us learn more about ourselves. It is even possible to use unpleasant emotions such as hate, jealousy, and shame to understand ourselves better and help other people. But that takes hard work.

Anger is a difficult and uncomfortable emotion for most people. Women, in particular, often consider their anger a destructive force that can spoil relationships and push away people who are important to them. Women are frequently afraid to tell a friend, a husband, or a child that they are angry, because they think that feeling anger is incompatible with feeling love and nurturance and caring.

In fact, anger can be a constructive emotion that helps resolve hurts and differences between people, improves their understanding of one another, and gives their relationships a firmer base. But this can happen only if we are willing to share our angry feelings with people who can help us rather than with those for whom the anger could be a terrible hurt.

Betty felt furious with her father for accepting a new job that paid less than the old one, on which the family had lived well. Ed had changed jobs because he had gone as far as he could at the old company and saw better opportunity for advancement at the new one. Before moving over, he discussed the situation with his wife and two teenage children, and they had all agreed that they could tighten their belts for one or two years with the expectation that things would be better later. Betty herself had encouraged her father's decision, because it seemed that the new job would also be more interesting, but after just a few months of a lower allowance and tightened budgets, she became angrier and angrier at him.

Betty did not want to hurt her father, and knew that she had participated in the decision that led to the current situation. Expressing her anger at her father after he had tried so hard to let the whole family make the decision, and at a time when he was working very hard and worried about whether he had done the right thing, would have been a destructive way of handling her anger. Betty struggled with the impulse to let him know how he had let her down, but suddenly decided to talk things over with her mother and sister instead. It turned out that they all felt angry, and also guilty at feeling that way, and together they came up with ways of handling their feelings so that they could continue to give Ed the support he needed.

Shame is also an unpleasant emotion, and one that we are often reluctant and afraid to share even with those closest to us. Some people find ways of using their shame to help others and end up feeling better about themselves in the process. At age forty-six, Bernice felt ashamed that she had never finished high school because her family had been poor and needed the money she could bring in by going to work as soon as she turned sixteen. She felt so ashamed that she lied on any forms or applications she filled out, and doing that added guilt to her already bad feelings. She had even hidden the truth from most of her friends.

Bernice's shame about failing to complete high school was also tied to the shame she felt as a child about being poor. Because of these experiences, she had married carefully, and her husband supported her and her two children well. Not wanting her daughters to repeat her "mistake," Bernice made certain that they finished high school and started college. Shortly after managing that, she took a job with an agency that counseled teenagers who had dropped out of school. She felt particularly qualified to talk to them about how their decision would affect the rest of their lives. Bernice found her work very satisfying and was especially excited when one of her clients decided to return to school.

Just as unpleasant emotions can be channeled constructively, so pleasant emotions can be used destructively. Even love for another person can be destructive when we permit it to consume us and push away our feelings for friends and family. At age twenty-one, Madeleine fell deeply in love with a man she met at work. She wanted to be with him constantly, and stopped seeing her friends and doing other activities. For three months John was her whole life, until he felt so oppressed he could no longer stand the relationship. "Twenty-four hours a day of the same person is just too much," he screamed at Madeleine during a fight. "I can't breathe and must get out to see other people." Sadly for Madeleine, the relationship ended because she did not know how to moderate her strong feelings of love, nor how to give her partner some independence from her.

Anxiety, a warning signal that something frightening or threatening is about to occur, can also be used constructively or destructively. For some of us, anxiety before an exam or a deadline at work makes us study that much harder to reduce the unpleasant feelings by learning enough to pass the exam or by meeting the deadline early. But others handle the anxiety by running away from the threatening situation and may go so far as to drop out of school because they have not found constructive ways to use anxiety as a warning signal. Instead of putting anxiety to work for them, they permit it to overwhelm them.

Some emotions, such as joy, might be easier to use constructively than others, such as hate. In any case, we learn to use feelings for our benefit and the benefit of others as we grow up and become able to think about how we feel and choose ways of expressing ourselves and acting on those feelings. Growing up includes developing more varied ways for using our emotions. We might say that our repertoire of methods for handling our feelings increases with experience.

SHORT-CIRCUITING OUR EMOTIONS

Sometimes we short-circuit our emotions, something we are usually unaware of doing. In a sense, part of us chooses *not to have our emotions.* These are times when a friend may ask, "Aren't you even angry at your boss for doing that?" and we honestly answer, "No." We do not feel angry, although everyone else expects us to.

Emotions enrich our lives, but they can also be scary and upsetting. Our own unique experiences with our emotions and how they affected others as we grew up may make feeling sad or envious or guilty so unpleasant that we short-circuit the feeling before we even become aware of it. Some of us do this only with certain feelings—anger, for instance. But there are people who more regularly short-circuit their emotions and are left without much feeling for most of the time. These people not only lose out on all the enjoyment we get from our emotions, but they may also find it difficult to build relationships with others because they cannot use their feelings to connect themselves with other people.

Short-circuiting our emotions takes its toll on us in other ways too. Sometimes we cannot label or understand feelings that come from past experiences but that are stirred up by what happens today. These feelings may be translated into real physical illness and be expressed in ways we least expect: a headache instead of anger, fatigue instead of sadness. When we short-circuit our emotions psychologically, our body sometimes takes over and expresses them for us.

Ginger suffered from exactly this problem but did not know it. For years she had endured headaches that became more and more severe—so bad that she needed an injection of a strong painkiller from her doctor each time one came on. Her doctor became concerned when Ginger began to come to him three times a week for this problem. Over the years, he had run every kind of medical test imaginable and could find nothing physically wrong with Ginger, but he knew that her headaches were real and that they came on at unexpected times.

The doctor recommended that Ginger talk with a mental-health counselor in another part of the clinic, because he suspected the headaches could be caused by something psychological. This turned out to be true. After meeting for a few months with a psychologist, Ginger realized how angry she was with her husband for carrying on an affair with his secretary of many years. Afraid that he would end the marriage, she had never mentioned it to him. In fact, she thought she had "accepted" it and never even felt angry about it. Unknowingly, she had endured the headaches instead.

The psychologist helped her talk to her husband about the situation, which was very difficult for her to do. She told her husband how she had tried to accept his wishes but that she had suffered greatly because of it. Her husband had thought that she had accepted his life-style and was shocked to hear that the terrible headaches that had upset both of them so much were part of her unfelt anger toward him. After a few months and a few joint meetings with the psychologist, Ginger's husband refused to drop the secretary and Ginger made the painful decision to separate from him, perhaps eventually to divorce. Her headaches had already begun to subside once she began to talk openly with her husband about the affair.

Sometimes the body takes over the role of expressing emotions because body and mind are not separate entities but work together to produce what we feel. Gail, for instance, worked for twenty years at a job from which she would be forced to retire in just six months when she turned sixty-five. She had loved her work and the people she worked with, and losing the job would mean losing her daily contact with them.

Despite this, Gail told herself and her co-workers how much she looked forward to retirement, and she began to plan her new life. This became more and more difficult as retirement approached because of how tired Gail felt. In contrast to her usual energetic and productive self, she felt fatigued and began to go to bed as soon as she arrived home from work. A checkup by her doctor showed that she was in excellent health and left her even more puzzled about her lack of energy.

Gail stopped attending church activities and barely made it to church on Sunday mornings. Her minister noticed this and phoned her to see how she was doing. They scheduled a time later in the week to have coffee together and talk. The minister listened to Gail talk about her enthusiasm for retirement without mentioning the loss of work and friends she had loved. He wondered about her omission, and decided to share with her his feelings about his own upcoming retirement.

"I feel two ways about it," he told Gail quietly. "I'm looking forward to more time with my wife and children and grandchildren, and more time to think and read and fish. But after all these years in this church with these people, I also feel very sad that I will not be here every day and that church members will no longer need me the way they have. Do you feel sad about leaving your friends at work?"

This question brought Gail to tears about all she was losing, and she and the minister together shared the sadness of retirement. She saw him again the following week, when they talked more about this, and Gail then began to share her sad feelings with co-workers, friends, and family. Sharing these feelings helped so much that

Gail gradually regained her usual energy and was able to plan actively for how she would spend her time after retirement.

Feelings enrich our lives and help us develop close connections with other people. It is difficult to escape having feelings, so if we don't want our feelings, they are bound to come out in surprising ways. Some women are so frightened of their feelings and their potential impact that they go through life without much feeling themselves, or much understanding of the intense feelings that other people often have. These women may not be unhappy, but they miss out on the richness and pleasure that others enjoy. We probably all know at least one person like this and may find it difficult to break through and become emotionally connected with him or her. These people often like to think that they use their minds more and are not at the mercy of their emotions.

Accepting our emotions and choosing constructive ways to use them is not easy. None of us does it perfectly, and most of us struggle constantly with how best to handle our feelings. In the end, struggling with them and using them can be most pleasant and rewarding. It is also the most human.

CHAPTER 2

Common Emotions

SADNESS, GRIEF, AND DEPRESSION: DIFFERENT FEELINGS FOR DIFFERENT TIMES

At times it may be difficult to tell some feelings from others because their outward signs can be similar. For instance, we may cry when we feel *sad* that we cannot afford handsome enough presents for our child's first Christmas. We may also cry when we feel *grief* over the death of a friend or loved one. We may cry, too, when we feel *depressed* about goals we had hoped for but have not been able to achieve—like a long-awaited promotion at work.

Feelings of sadness, grief, and depression are linked by other outward signs too. We may lose interest in our usual activities, find ourselves moping around the house, or lack energy for friends and fun. Despite these commonalities, sadness, grief, and depression represent different types of responses to events and people in our lives.

All these feelings can be a normal part of everyday life. We cannot have everything in life that we would like to have or expect to have, and we may feel sad when we realize this. Nor can we have all the peace and fulfillment most of us desire. It is inevitable, and human, that we feel sad about this.

Kitty and her family lived for seven years in an old house on a small plot of land they had worked hard to turn into a garden that flowered almost every month of the year. Most of the street facing their home had been a woods and meadow vivid with wild flowers every spring for as long as neighbors could remember. Two summers ago, the owners of the property across the street decided to sell, and a developer immediately bought the land, planning to remake Kitty's lovely view into six identical houses. The town council resolved the fight between the block's residents and the builder by issuing a permit for five houses.

The whole neighborhood felt sad about the impending loss of the "street forest" they had assumed would be there forever. At first Kitty tried to save some of the wild flowers, wild quince, and strawberries by transplanting, but they did not seem to take. Kitty cried a bit each day as the developers cut down more and more of the trees. By fall, with the foundations of the new houses going in, pangs of sadness had lessened, and she began to feel curious about who the new neighbors might be.

But it would be simplifying too much to say that Kitty felt only sadness. She also felt grief at the loss of the meadow and woods. We feel grief when we lose something—hope, a person we cared about, a goal we expected to achieve. In this sense, Kitty felt not only sad but also grieved over the loss of her beloved street forest.

Kitty's feelings were not that different from those of Marsha, who frequently felt sad about the wars and violent conflicts she read about in the newspaper every morning. Sometimes she cried as she read the stories. Events thousands of miles away saddened her, as events across the street saddened Kitty.

Feelings of sadness, while they may stay with us for a while, do not usually interfere with our daily work or obligations. We continue to get up in the morning, to take care of our families, to go to our jobs, and to meet the usual demands of our lives. Grief, on the other hand, may interfere more with our everyday life, particularly if we have lost a person who was close to us. Sometimes people feel ashamed to show grief openly or to let others know how painful it will be to go on without the important person they lost.

But grief, and its outward signs of crying and sadness, is a normal part of human life. When we grieve over a loss, we let ourselves and others know how attached we were to another person, and that is exactly what human life is about: getting attached to and caring about other people.

Sometimes grieving for another person may continue a long time. A husband or a wife, or a parent or a child, may spend several months grieving over the loss of the other. Even the faintest reminder of things that brought pleasure to the lost person—a crunchy fall leaf, a cup of hot peppermint tea—can quickly bring back feelings of grief. There are times when grieving goes on privately, so that if you are suffering a loss, you may want to stay home from work for a few days or a week and spend time with family or close friends who share your feelings. Sometimes the loss of a loved one may make sleeping or eating difficult for months and it takes time to get back to usual patterns. Resuming regular activities, however, can sometimes help us feel better faster.

Depression often looks like sadness and grief because some of the outward signs are similar. When we are depressed we feel sad, we may cry, we may lose our appetites and not feel like eating, and we may have trouble sleeping. Depression comes in different forms. From time to time, most of us experience "the blues," a transient variety of depression that gets us feeling down when we may not even understand why.

Donna, for example, felt very happy when she and her boyfriend decided to get married. She called her parents and friends to share the good news and began planning her wedding. But after the first few weeks of excitement, Donna lost her energy and began to feel blue whenever she thought about marriage or planning the ceremony. She and Bob had known each other for a long time, and they loved each other, so Donna's sudden lack of enthusiasm confused her.

Things became clearer for Donna when she had several conversations with a recently married friend about the freedom *she* had lost by getting married—despite how happy the marriage had made her. She realized that she had felt blue because marrying meant gaining as well as losing and at thirty she would have to adjust to being tied to another person.

While Donna's blues did not interfere with her everyday life, more serious depression can. The outward signs of serious depression may be a more intense variety of the outward signs of sadness or transient blues: crying and difficulty sleeping and eating. In more severe depression, a woman may feel unable to carry out her usual work, whether it's taking care of her family or going to a job. She may have no energy, want to stay in bed, and lose interest in people and events around her.

Hallmarks of depression are unrealistic and distorted ways of thinking which, by themselves, may lead to some of the sad feelings that accompany depression. A depressed woman, for instance, may evaluate herself as a failure and things that happen to her as unpleasant when in fact they are not. Meredith thought this way when she was fortunate enough to be offered a good job after competition with many other applicants. She accepted the job, but instead of attributing her good fortune to her special talents, she believed that her new employers had made a mistake in hiring her, a mistake they would soon discover. She believed that the other applicants were more experienced and that she did not deserve the job. These thoughts made what would be a happy occasion for most people a depressing one for Meredith. She was convinced that she would be fired soon after starting work. Such errors in thinking usually do not occur along with feelings of normal sadness and grief and therefore are hallmarks of depression.

There are other differences between sadness, grief, and the blues, on the one hand, and depression on the other. A depressed woman often feels she is worthless, and sometimes she feels guilty about events over which she has little control. She may also have trouble concentrating and making decisions and find that her thinking is slower than usual. She may not feel as "sharp" as she used to. Most serious, a severely depressed woman may think of hurting herself or wish to be dead.

Severe depression can be due, at least partly, to an imbalance in brain biochemistry. Such a condition can last as long as six months if not treated with drugs and psychotherapy. Whereas sadness, grief, and the blues are normal in everyday life, severe depression is an emotional illness for which professional help may be urgent, especially if a woman is thinking of suicide.

Depression comes in various shapes and sizes, sometimes more severe than transient blues but sometimes less serious than the very severe variety that can include thoughts of suicide. It is not always easy to tell the difference between sadness or grief or the blues, and severe depression. Sometimes they slide into one another so that, little by little, a woman grieving over the death of her husband slips into a more serious depression that requires the help of a mental-health professional.

Maryanne found herself in exactly this situation. She felt grief-stricken and lost after the death of her husband of forty-one years. For the first few weeks, she stopped going out to her usual card club, the movies, and on shopping trips with friends. She even discouraged visits from close friends and her two children because she said she wanted to spend some time alone with her husband's memory. But by the end of a month of this kind of grieving, Maryanne had lost eleven pounds and rarely got out of bed. She thought more and more about "joining Jim" by killing herself with the sleeping pills prescribed by her family doctor. When she mentioned this to her daughter, her daughter insisted that she see a psychotherapist to talk about how bad she was feeling.

FEAR AND ANXIETY: WARNING SIGNS

We all probably remember feeling afraid of the dark as children when we could not see what was going on around us. Just as such fears are common among children, there are adult fears that many of us share too. Fear of nuclear war is a common adult fear today.

But many fears are idiosyncratic to each of us as individuals. Diana, for instance, feels terrified of riding in cars because of an accident she experienced as a young child when her father skidded on a wet road and slammed into a tree. Fortunately no one was hurt, but the severe impact was very scary to a seven-year-old child. At twenty-eight, Diana still has not learned how to drive.

Feeling afraid of something is a signal that we should avoid that situation. Fear is one way we protect ourselves from potentially dangerous events. We feel afraid to walk in high-crime neighborhoods at night, and that feeling keeps us from doing it and from getting hurt. But some idiosyncratic fears, such as Diana's fear of cars, can be more intense than the real danger and make our lives difficult.

It is not always easy to distinguish between realistic fears that protect us from harm and fears that arise from special occurrences in our lives. Diana's fear of riding in or driving an automobile is one example, because current statistics show that cars *are* dangerous, that they can hurt or kill. Yet most people drive. Fears protect us from harm, but they can also interfere with our lives. Fears represent a trade-off between the possibility of injury and restriction on our life.

One test of whether a fear is worth holding on to because it protects us is to think about how much the fear itself affects our lives. Staying away from a high-crime neighborhood may not interfere at all with the things we want to do, especially since it is a fear that we probably share with many friends. No one wants to go there, so we do not miss out on dates or parties or trips. But being afraid to ride in an automobile may greatly affect our everyday lives, particularly if we live in an area where there is little public transportation. It may cause us to turn down invitations from friends, to give up visits to relatives, or to lose out on a good job. Rather than acting as a warning sign that protects us from injury, this type of *psychological fear* may be protecting us from bad memories instead.

Anxiety also acts as a protective signal, but instead of protecting us from physical harm, anxiety protects us from psychological harm or hurt. The overwhelming anxiety we may feel before a party—so intense that it keeps us at home—may be insulating us from the rejection we expect once we get there.

While we usually know it when we feel fear, anxiety can mask itself in a variety of forms so that we do not always know that it is anxiety we are experiencing. In fact, different people experience anxiety in different

ways. For some it is butterflies in the stomach, for others
it is nervous hands that drop everything they touch. For
others, anxiety can mean feeling dazed and preoccupied
and constantly forgetting what they have set out to do.
Anxiety shows itself in many forms, from vague and
uncomfortable feelings in our bodies to difficulty concentrating and thinking.

Whatever form it takes, anxiety is there to protect us
from psychological harm. Just as fear signals a physical
threat, anxiety lets us know that a psychological threat is
imminent. It keeps us away from potentially dangerous
situations, situations that could make us feel stupid,
rejected, unsure of ourselves, angry, or out of control. But
just like fear protects unnecessarily at times and restricts
our lives, so anxiety can be an overreaction to a situation
that may have hurt us in the past.

While a teenager, Tom attended a football game at
which some opposing fans picked a fight with him and
his friends. The fight unleashed Tom's anger so intensely that it frightened him. He felt out of control as he
aggressively fought the other boys. Ever since, attending
football games has made Tom feel shaky. Sometimes his
knees feel so weak that he is not sure he can walk from
his car to the stadium. But Tom, now thirty years old,
does not link these feelings with his experience as an
eighteen-year-old and cannot figure out what it is about
football games that makes him feel so "weird." His
anxiety is a disconnected remnant of that earlier experience with his own intense anger out of control, and the
anxiety protects him from situations in which he might
feel that way again.

Although fear protects us from physical hurts, and
anxieties protect us from psychological hurts, they can
both restrict our lives in extreme ways. Sometimes the
pain they cause is greater than the pain they protect us
from. For example, mild or moderate anxiety about

getting good grades on tests protects us from failure by forcing us to study. But severe anxiety about failure can keep us out of school altogether. That would protect us from failure, but it also would seriously handicap our lives.

ANGER: A SPECIAL PROBLEM FOR WOMEN

Anger is one of the most difficult emotions for women to accept in themselves and to express. Feeling angry tells us that we have been hurt by another person, that something is wrong. We feel angry when our husband fails to praise our efforts to prepare a special meal on a day that he had a rough meeting scheduled with his boss. We feel angry when we are passed over for a much-deserved promotion for a co-worker who has not been there as long. We feel angry when our children do not seem to appreciate the extra things we do to make them happy.

We feel hurt and angry when these things happen, but at the same time we feel unsure about whether we are *entitled* to be angry. After all, our husband worked hard that day—too hard, we tell ourselves, to say thank you for the unusual meal—and will get angry himself if we complain about his lack of compliments. And our children *deserve* to be taken care of and made comfortable. That's what mothers are for!

One thing that makes it so hard for us to allow ourselves to be angry—and to express our anger—is the belief that women are supposed to take care of people. In fact, we often define our lives by what we do for others as daughters, sisters, wives, and mothers. If we get angry, we may not do such a good job. How can an angry person take care of others? We have learned to ignore our anger, to accumulate it, instead of feeling it and expressing it.

The special nature of women's lives also makes expressing anger difficult. Jean Baker Miller, a psychiatrist who specializes in the psychology of women, explains that relationships with other people have always been central to women. This is as true of modern women with careers outside the home as it is of women who have chosen to be full-time homemakers. For both groups, connectedness with others—children, husbands, parents, friends—plays an important role in their lives.

Karen faced this dilemma. She had become close to her supervisor, Nora, at work. In addition to working well together, they often ate lunch together and shared stories about their families and future plans. Despite their closeness, Nora never praised Karen for her work. Karen would often overhear her complimenting others, and she felt that she was doing just as good a job. She felt more and more hurt and more and more angry, but she didn't dare bring up her feelings with Nora because she feared losing the friendship that meant so much to her.

Finally, when Nora praised another worker right in front of Karen, it upset her enough that she left work and went to the gym. A good swimmer, she felt that endless laps in the pool would help ease her hurt and fury. By the time she was exhausted from swimming, her anger was also exhausted, and she returned to work feeling much calmer. Swimming three times a week became a must for Karen during the years she spent at this job.

According to Dr. Miller, women develop many psychological strengths from their need for closeness: the capacity to be empathic with the feelings of others, to be emotionally in tune with other people, to know how to comfort others when they are hurt. But when expression of anger is seen as potentially dangerous, the need for closeness also inhibits their ability to express that emotion. Expression of anger may disrupt a relationship that is crucial to a woman's feelings of well-being. It may threaten the existence of a relationship on which a woman depends heavily. At these times, a woman may believe that feelings of anger must be avoided at all cost.

But it is not just women's special role as caretakers of other people, or their strong need for connectedness, that makes feelings of anger and expressing anger so difficult for women. Common stereotypes in our culture about femininity and the ideal woman add to our problems with anger. To many people, femininity means being cooperative, compliant, and "ladylike," a pattern of behavior that hardly leaves room for angry feelings. When we reject anger as part of femininity, we reject an emotion that is a natural part of human life.

Given their special role as caretakers, women's strong need for connectedness, and a view of femininity that does not leave room for acceptance of or expression of anger, it is no wonder that women feel uncertain about angry feelings and how to express and act on them. Men sometimes have trouble expressing their feelings too, but the feelings they have trouble with are different. For example, men may find it difficult to admit to feeling afraid, or even to let themselves feel fear, but they usually allow themselves to feel anger and to let people know it. Men can also express anger through competitive games and competition in work. These differences have their roots in the ways we raise boys and girls. While our ideal of femininity excludes the chance to feel and act angry, our ideal of masculinity calls for aggressiveness, competitiveness, and strength, and we rear our children according to these expectations.

Because we tend to prohibit feelings and actions of anger in women, they tend to accumulate instead of getting out in healthy ways. Leah, for example, had been a happily married homemaker for twenty-one years when she began to feel blue and tired much of the time. Her husband and two teenage children had always been appreciative of the way she took care of them, and their love and gratefulness made her happy and sustained her efforts. But now, nothing they said to her seemed enough, and she lost interest in taking care of them at all. She stopped cooking meals, inviting the children's friends, and planning their much-enjoyed vacations.

As Leah felt worse and worse, her family became worried and encouraged her to talk to a psychologist. At their first meeting, Leah began to cry, but it was not long before she realized how much she wanted someone to take care of her. She and the psychologist met for a few months while Leah discovered how angry she felt toward her "wonderful family" who had always carefully thanked her for taking care of them but never offered to take care of her in return. "If someone would just offer to get me a cup of tea when I'm tired, it would mean a lot," she told the counselor.

Leah had been very good at taking care of others and very good at ignoring the anger that had been accumulating over not getting taken care of herself. The anger had turned inward and used up all the energy, enthusiasm, and love she had been giving them.

When we keep ourselves from feeling or expressing our anger, it accumulates, and we either turn it inward as Leah did or suddenly explode, much to the surprise of ourselves and others. Anger is an inevitable part of being human and of having relationships with others. People invariably say or do things that hurt, and anger is a natural reaction to these experiences. Sometimes it is hard for us to *find* our anger, let alone express it, but if we do not look for it and assume it's not there or will go away, it will just get worse, making things more difficult for us and for the people we are close to. Expressing anger not only provides relief for ourselves, it can also help other people see things differently. Expressing anger relieves hurt and can change things.

LOVE: NOT ALWAYS AS EASY AS IT LOOKS

Love is the emotion that brings us the greatest happiness and satisfaction. When we love other people, we enjoy being with them, watching them, sharing with them. We care about them, and our own well-being is tied to theirs. Loving others means that we like them, but it goes beyond liking to deep feelings that come from our innermost selves. Sometimes we choose the people we love—our husbands, our boyfriends, our close female friends—but at other times we love people simply because of who they are: parents and children. Feelings of love can at times be quite powerful and greatly affect our lives. The common phrase "falling in love" suggests how helpless we may feel in the face of such a strong emotion that may overpower us.

To many of us, love feels "magic," because we often cannot describe precise reasons for loving someone or, if we can, the reasons themselves do not add up to how intensely we feel. Because of this, we may attribute love to "the right chemistry," a set of unknown factors that lead to deep attachment. In fact, a "psychological chemistry" probably lies behind our special feelings of love. Psychologists and psychiatrists think that the chemistry comes from our experiences as infants and children as we were loved by and in turn loved our parents. These experiences are unique to each of us, and we do not remember them, but they affect our choice of the people we fall in love with as adults.

While the chemistry may overwhelm us at first when we are choosing a mate, romantic love itself does not usually last very long. It can, however, form the foundation for a life of caring, commitment, and joy. Romantic love can turn into deep and long-lasting feelings for our partner. In fact, it is our commitment to another person and our concern about that person's well-being which are the hallmarks of love and which differentiate love from romance, infatuation, and "puppy love."

Over years and years, though, it may be difficult to feel committed and concerned—to love—all the time. Loving another person is rarely always positive, and there will be times when we feel burdened by or angry with that person and may want to stay alone more. These times are often difficult for people who love each other, because we expect that "love is always," when in fact it is not. No one is perfect, and there may be times when we will be especially sensitive to our loved one's imperfections. It is impossible to love another person *all* the time without occasionally having ambivalent feelings. This does not mean we no longer love the person—it's just the natural way love comes out.

Feelings of ambivalence toward people we love may be particularly difficult for women for whom love is tied up with the desire to take care of other people. Women express their love through nurturance, support, and care-taking, and we may become upset when we suddenly do not feel like fulfilling these roles. We may wonder if we still love our families when taking care of them has unexpectedly become burdensome instead of joyful. Women may consider themselves selfish if they do not feel like giving the nurturance they and others expect them to provide.

Annette experienced this problem after ten years of a happy marriage and five-year-old twin girls. She was a lawyer who worked three days a week in a local firm because she felt she needed to use the professional training she had worked so hard to attain. Annette enjoyed her work, and she also enjoyed taking care of husband and children when she was at home. They seemed to be a happy family, but Annette had developed growing feelings of resentment about taking care of her husband and twins, about having to spend all her out-of-the-office hours with them. She began to wonder if she still loved them.

Eventually Annette decided to share her feelings with her husband. He immediately felt hurt that his wife had lost interest in the family. After several discussions, both he and Annette realized that they loved each other as much as always, but that they had conflicting ideas about how that love should be expressed. They tried one solution after another. First they went away separately a few weekends a year: Annette to visit women friends in other cities or to spend a few days alone on a beach, and Bob to go fishing more often or to spend some weekends home alone with the twins. When that did not seem to help, Annette tried working full-time, but that just made her more tired and resentful. Despite their love, they had a lot of trouble coming up with a way to live together more comfortably.

Because of the way boys and girls are usually raised, some women and men have learned to express love in different ways. While for women love is tied to caretaking and nurturance, to men it may mean the capacity to support and protect their loved ones. Things are changing now. Women are working more and contributing to the financial support of their families. And men have begun to realize all the satisfaction and joy they have missed by emphasizing work and not participating in raising children. In some couples, men and women are beginning to show their love in more similar ways.

Loving another person will sometimes call for giving up something we want in order that our loved ones can be happy or comfortable. A wife and mother, happy in her hometown, may be asked to move to a strange city to further her husband's career. She may be able to make this sacrifice out of love as long as her husband appreciates it and seems willing to make sacrifices on her behalf

when the time comes. Giving to others is a central part of
the image women have of themselves, and their self-
esteem often depends on how well they live up to this
ideal. But because love and caretaking and giving are so
tied together for women, we may go overboard in letting
the interests of others come first. Sometimes we do this
out of fear that we will lose the love of children, husband,
or close friends if we act more in our own interest. Losing
love that is very important to us may feel like we are
losing our self, because women organize their lives
around connections with others.

But love cannot be fed by giving alone. A love relationship designed to take care of one person more than the
other, or to have one partner do most of the giving, will
eventually make one mate feel deprived and overbur-
dened. This is a trap that women's way of loving can
sometimes lead to. Even with our children, who for many
years are dependent on us for their very existence and
give back, in return, the joy of their lives and of watching
them live and grow, do not require constant giving in
order to thrive. In fact, too much sacrifice may eventually
make a mother too angry to enjoy the children completely.

Because love and taking care of other people play such
a crucial part in women's lives, women find it particularly troublesome when they do not feel love in situations
in which they expect it. Children are supposed to love
their parents, for instance, but painful experiences as we
grow up may hurt us so badly that we sometimes feel
unable to love parents as we think we should. This can
make us sad and guilty and be a loss for both parents and
children, whose bond could be a source of deep satisfaction throughout life.

When these tense situations do occur, we should try to
accept our feelings without guilt, because guilt merely
adds to the deprivation we already feel. Sometimes

broken or tense bonds of love are irreparable, and we may grieve their loss. But there are times as adults when we may feel ready to try to make amends, to accept our parents as they are, to love them in whatever way we can. This may occur later in adulthood, when the hurts of childhood have faded and have been eased by the joy and comfort of new loves and relationships.

Love is not an emotion to be reserved for family alone. As we go through life, we choose as friends people with whom we can share much that is intimate about ourselves and families. Women seem particularly talented at making and sustaining such friendships. We may begin these friendships because we meet someone we like or can talk to, or someone who shares the same interests— tennis or hiking, for example. Over the years, these may turn into deep attachments that include commitment and caring. Sometimes it is a best friend whose love sustains us through difficult times with our families.

JOY: SHARING WITH OTHERS

Joy is an emotion that makes the world look beautiful. When we feel joy, we often feel one with the world and with other people. Sometimes specific events bring us this emotion: love, success at work, a long-awaited special vacation. At other times we feel joy from more everyday occurrences: a sunny, warm day with buds on the trees that promise spring, a walk in the first snowfall of the year, a letter from a friend, the smile of an infant.

Joy is brought by experiences great and small. Adele remembers clearly the weeks of joy she spent in Florence, Italy, roaming among the great works of art preserved for centuries. She had chosen to go by herself because she had waited so long to see the treasures that she wanted no interference but merely to feel the joy of their beauty.

Other people feel that the best part of joy is sharing it with others. Milton and Kathy fondly remember their mule ride down the Grand Canyon because they took the bumps and turns together, laughing at the discomfort of the awesome trek past geological eons of time.

Joy is a special feeling, but it is not an everyday feeling. As young children, we may expect life to be constant excitement and joy, but it is not. People who have trouble adapting to this reality sometimes seek artificial methods of feeling joy. They may use drugs or excessive sex, or look for thrills with cars and outrageous escapades.

In real life, joy comes occasionally, and we are fortunate when it arrives. It is to be cherished as a special emotion.

GUILT AND SHAME: WE ARE NOT PERFECT

We feel guilty and ashamed when we think that we have failed to meet our own expectations or those of others. We may feel guilty that we have not loved our parents as much as we should have, that we have not spent as much time with our children as they might need, that we have not worked hard enough at our jobs, or that we have not shown enough devotion and love to God. When we feel shame, we want to hide what we think are failures or defects from others.

Both shame and guilt come from unmet expectations. Often we learn these standards from our parents when we are young. We may then set such high standards for ourselves that achieving them becomes virtually impossible. After all, no human being is perfect, so why should *we* expect to be that way?

Guilt and shame are uncomfortable feelings. Marjorie worked full-time as a social worker and spent less time with her husband and children than she thought she should. When she was growing up her mother did not work outside the home at all and was waiting for Marjorie and her brother when they arrived home from school. She prepared all the meals and took care of everything around the house. But with Marjorie working, both her husband and children had to chip in and help with housework and dinner. Because Marjorie felt so guilty about the way things worked out, she gave the children extra spending money and let them buy more playthings than she ordinarily would, to make up for what she felt was inadequate time as a mother.

Marjorie's solution to feelings of guilt is not unusual. Since women are supposed to take care of other people, it is not uncommon for us to feel that we have not done enough. After all, there is no end to what other people need, and we cannot satisfy everyone completely, not even our infants and children. Feelings of guilt can affect relationships in harmful ways. We may buy off our children, sacrifice ourselves for our families, or encourage colleagues for promotion at work rather than ourselves.

When we feel guilty, it is a signal that we have reached our unique limits for how to act, how to work, or how to love, and that we are dissatisfied with these limits. Learning to accept the limits of our energy and capacity is hard, but it is a much more comfortable resolution of guilty feelings than trying to keep going in different and exhausting ways.

The kinds of things we feel guilty about are unique to us and usually come from our parents' expectations of us as children, experiences we had with other people, and the way people around us behaved. If we saw our mother take care of her own elderly parents, we ourselves may expect to do that, and feel guilty if we cannot meet that expectation as adults.

As we grow up our parents teach us how to behave and expect us to act in certain ways. As adults, we may feel guilty or ashamed if we fail them by acting differently or setting limits on how much we give to others. It is not easy to throw off the things we have learned as children, but new learning can take place when we become involved with other people—husbands or close friends, for example—with whom we can talk over our mutual expectations and limits.

Not all our expectations and standards come from our parents. Some come from the customs of the society we live in. We may feel guilty and ashamed if we fail to meet these public expectations. For instance, stealing and cheating are unacceptable, and even if no one notices, we may feel privately ashamed when we violate such prohibitions.

At other times, we feel ashamed because we have broken what we think are unspoken rules and customs of our society. In America, television, movies, magazines, and commercials tell us we are supposed to be rich, beautiful, elegantly dressed, always in love, and having fun with lots of friends. Very, very few people meet all these ideals. Nonetheless, these expectations make some of us ashamed of being poor, or short, or driving an old car, or having fun only on those rare occasions when work and chores are done.

Shame—especially this private kind that makes us feel we are not quite as good as other people, even though we have not violated the morals of our society—can be very hurtful. We may feel that we are not a worthy woman because we are not beautiful enough, smart enough, thin enough. Our self-esteem may suffer if we believe the images and ideals offered by the mass media. These images and ideals have been developed in order to shame us into buying goods that the message tells us beautiful and rich people buy.

We have pointed out that certain people can stir up unpleasant feelings. While we sometimes feel guilty and ashamed when we fail to act according to certain ideals—private, public, moral, or legal—we may also feel these emotions whenever we are around certain people. This may at first seem mysterious to us.

Gwen, for example, was a happy twenty-five-year-old law student who had just one year of school left and looked forward to graduation and work. An only child, she came from a poor family, and college and law school had been financially difficult for parents and child. But they had accepted the burden proudly—Gwen working summers and her parents at extra jobs—because she was to be the first lawyer in their family. Gwen never felt guilty about the extra work her parents had to put in, because she knew how much pride they took in her accomplishments. She also realized that, as a lawyer, she would make enough money to share with them.

But Gwen had an aunt—her father's sister—who could not understand how the family could feel happy with the arrangements they had made. Every time she saw Gwen, she did not miss the opportunity to make her niece feel guilty and ashamed at what she was "putting her parents through." Aunt Bess chided Gwen at Christmas, at Thanksgiving, at Easter, and at all the other times Gwen visited the lonely aunt whom she loved and had been so attached to as a child. Gwen would arrive for her visits looking forward to seeing Aunt Bess, but after just a few minutes she would feel hurt, guilty, and ashamed over the family's choice.

Gwen endured this during three years of law school because she did not want to argue with her favorite aunt and because she knew that she and her parents were happy with the agreement they had made. Not until several years after Gwen's graduation, when she began to make enough money to share with her parents, did

Bess realize how difficult she had been and apologized to her niece.

For some, nothing we can do is good enough, and they will make us feel guilty and ashamed no matter how hard we try or how much we offer. In these situations, guilt and shame arise from comparisons made by others about how we measure up to their expectations. Being around these people may always make us feel uncomfortable.

JEALOUSY AND ENVY:
HALF EMPTY OR HALF FULL

When we feel jealous or envious of other people, we believe that they have something we do not have, or that they have more than we do. We may feel jealousy and envy over something as simple as a pretty dress or something as complicated as a whole family. Feeling jealous and envious may also come from our own feelings of deprivation, of not having what we want, of not having enough for ourselves.

Jealousy and envy are as different as loving and liking. While envy of what someone else has may be transient and not affect our relationship with them, jealousy is usually longer-lasting and comes from our innermost feelings about ourselves and our lives. We envy other people's possessions or good fortune, but jealousy has more to do with our feelings about other people and our relationships with them.

Mary, for instance, often found herself envious of Grace's beautiful clothing. The two women were best friends, but Grace came from a wealthy family and could afford the kind of clothing that Mary could not. At times, however, the two women shopped together, with Mary enjoying watching Grace try on dress after dress until she found the right one. Mary was openly envious of Grace's good fortune, and the two women often joked about it when Mary wore the same dress to the theater twice in a row.

Mary's envy did not affect her closeness with Grace, nor did it make Mary feel deprived and cheated. She felt satisfied with her life, her family, and her work, and could accept the fact that she could not afford what her best friend easily could. Mary felt good enough about herself to tolerate differences between the two of them.

Jealousy, however, can be a more pernicious emotion that may deeply affect and even harm relationships that are important to us. While feelings of envy come from the common observation that some people around us have more of some things than we do, feelings of jealousy come from a more deep-seated sense of having been deprived ourselves. Feelings of envy thus require observation of what other people have, in fact, they depend on it. But feelings of jealousy do not even require that we see other people with more than we have. Feelings of jealousy depend more on how deprived we ourselves feel than how much other people really have.

There are always people who have more than we do: more money, more beauty, more success, more family life. These differences affect some of us more than others. Sometimes we may feel angry at the unfair way gifts have been given out at birth. We may feel so angry and so jealous and so hurt about the inequities that we forget to look at our own assets. Some people see themselves as half full with the good things of their lives. Others see themselves as half empty and lacking the good things that other people have. To be so jealous that we see ourselves as empty means we ignore the half that is full and all our assets that fill it.

Joann felt exactly this way. Even as a teenager, she had never felt satisfied with what her family had given her. She was always envious of friends whom she thought got more: better clothing, more expensive jewelry, more parties, fancier vacations. Joann felt deprived compared to what other people seemed to have, and her jealousy continued through college, where it made it difficult for her to make friends. She couldn't bear to be with women who seemed to have more than she did. Joann felt increasingly resentful, and these situations grew more and more painful for her. Women wanted to be friends, but she rejected one after the other.

Joann finally did fall in love, and her intensely jealous feelings persisted through her relationship with her boyfriend, whom she expected to fill her half-empty self. But even he could not do that, and after months of trying and fighting, they went to see a counselor who specialized in such problems. At last Joann began to understand how deprived she had felt as a child—not of clothes and cars and parties, but of affection. All these years she had tried to make up for what she had missed in the wrong ways.

Joann's jealousy was so intense that it made her unhappy for years and made it difficult for her to have friends. It also helped her ignore her real assets: her engaging personality, her sense of humor, her athletic abilities. One of the most harmful effects of jealousy is that it prevents us from fully appreciating ourselves and our strengths. When jealous, we focus instead on what we lack.

HATE: THE OTHER SIDE OF LOVE

Hate is an emotion that can be as intense as love. Both feelings come from, and touch, our innermost selves. But aside from the striking similarities in their source and in the intensity of their feeling and expression, hate and love are in fact emotional opposites. In love we see the best of another person. We invest ourselves in that best and want to take care of it, nurture it, be with it. In hate we see the worst in another person, and rather than taking it into ourselves to nurture and enjoy, we take it in to demean it and disdain it.

When we feel hate, we are not just rejecting a person whom we will later ignore. When we merely reject people, we have decided that we do not like them enough to be friends, that they are "not our type," or that they live too far away to be able to maintain a relationship. Kate and Jeff met at a conference in Chicago and hit it off well, spending time together after conference hours. But Jeff lived in Chicago and Kate lived in New York. Both had good jobs, families, and friends in their home cities, and neither could conceive of moving. They decided that despite their attraction for each other, things could not work out, and they separated sadly when the conference ended. After a few weeks, each had just about forgotten the other as they became involved with other people.

Dora had a different experience with rejection. She met a woman at her new job who wanted to be friends, but Dora already had a lot of friends and felt too busy to become involved with still another one that she did not like very much. So, as nicely and as often as she could, she told Nancy that she was busy when Nancy asked about doing things together. Eventually Nancy got the hint and began to make friends with other women in the office.

Neither Kate nor Dora hated Jeff or Nancy. Their feelings were simply not very intense, and the relationships never became important enough or close enough to invest their feelings in them.

Although hate is not an everyday emotion, most of us feel hate temporarily at various times, often toward people we are close to and very angry at. But hate can also be longer-lasting and more harmful. Sometimes it means that we invest heavily in another person with bad feelings rather than with the good feelings love usually brings. Just as love takes a lot of our time and energy and preoccupies us, keeping us from concentrating on other things, so hatred may also rob us of our energy for other people and other work. Like love, it may be all-consuming.

When we feel hate toward someone, it is usually because we feel that they have hurt us in some terrible way, perhaps even maliciously and on purpose. People are sometimes cruel to each other, and their actions and words can cause us to hate them.

Molly, for example, had always been mean to her older sister, of whom she felt very jealous. She believed that because Nina was more beautiful she was treated better at home and at school, always getting extra goodies, praise, and love. Nina, in turn, alienated Molly with her beauty and success, refusing to include her in parties and dates and acting unfriendly at every opportunity. Molly grew up hating her sister, and her hate affected everything in her life: her schoolwork, her lack of interest in men, her fears of rejection, her shyness.

Molly needed help with her bad feelings, but so did Nina, who, instead of reaching out to love her less successful younger sister, used her beauty against her.

At other times when we feel hate it is not because another person's actions led us to hate them but rather because of something in ourselves that might lead us to hate certain people. This is not too different from the psychological chemistry of love. Sometimes we are attracted intensely to people because of very early but forgotten experiences with love while growing up. We may also love people for what they stand for or for what they fulfilled in our lives that we have missed or feel deprived of.

Similarly, we may grow to hate a person who stirs up early and forgotten experiences with the people who took care of us as infants and children. In these instances, psychological chemistry can lead to hate just as it can lead to love.

Margot had exactly this experience with her new boss, Phil, and could not figure out what it was about him that upset her so intensely that she hated him and her job too, only months after starting. Just talking to the boss stirred her up, making her feel that she wanted to move away. She had to force herself to go to his office for the weekly staff meetings. And at the slightest provocation, Margot would become furious and retreat to a corner to sulk. She found it hard even to speak to Phil politely. She had begun by liking her work, but her intense response to the boss made her less enthusiastic. Eventually he decided they could not work together and asked her to resign. Margot was upset, but also relieved.

Hate is a difficult and powerful emotion, because we usually believe that we are not supposed to hate people, that we are not supposed to feel hate at all. But we are imperfect beings, and the capacity to hate is one of our imperfections. Sometimes all we can do is accept these powerful feelings in ourselves and look toward friends or family for help, reassurance, and guidance.

Feelings of hate may be even more difficult to deal with when we experience them in situations in which we might usually feel love. We are expected, and in fact commanded by God, to love our parents. But there may be times when we hate them. For some of us, growing up was difficult, and we did not receive the kind of help we needed from our parents. As adults, we may feel hatred toward one or both of our parents for their failings as guides into adult life. Feeling hate is painful and can eat away at whatever good feelings about life we do have, at whatever capacity we do have for love and joy. But feeling constant hatred toward people we are supposed to love—parents, children, or husband—can make all of life very difficult and unhappy.

Hatred is not limited to what we feel about other people. Sometimes we end up hating ourselves. This can be either transient or chronic. Feelings of self-hate can come from our failure to live up to unrealistic expectations, some learned while we were very young. They can also come from early experiences as infants and children.

Hate is a destructive emotion, perhaps the most destructive of all the feelings we have discussed. Not only can the person who is the object of the hate be hurt, but even more, we ourselves can be hurt. Hate leaves little room for other, happier emotions and little room for love. Self-hate is particularly pernicious because it can make it very difficult to let anyone come close to us, to let anyone love us.

WE RARELY EXPERIENCE JUST ONE EMOTION AT A TIME

Emotions usually come in pairs and triplets rather than one at a time. Rarely do we experience pure guilt or pure joy. Guilt mixed with anger and joy mixed with love are more common. In fact, we sometimes experience several conflicting emotions at once. They may not all occur at the same minute, but throughout the day or week we may experience many different emotions. Our feelings and the words that come with them may change.

Some emotions combine to produce still others over long periods of time. Feelings of anger and jealousy and deprivation may eventually harden into a bitterness about life that tinges everything we observe, feel, and experience. This will affect our outlook and our relationships with people.

Learning to accept ourselves as imperfect and our emotions as part of life will make life easier. We have each developed a style of handling the emotions that feel good or bad, the ones that are beautiful to others and the ones that are destructive. It is important to find constructive ways of handling our feelings, ways that are comfortable for us and for those around us.

CHAPTER 3

Coping with Our Emotions

HIDING AND SHARING OUR FEELINGS: THE IMPORTANCE OF CONNECTEDNESS

Some of the emotions discussed in Chapter 2 are easier to share with people, while others are more difficult. Love and joy, for example, are often naturally shared with others, whereas we may want to hide feelings of guilt, shame, or hatred. But it is not the type of emotion alone that influences the ease or difficulty of sharing. We each vary considerably in capacity and willingness to share our feelings.

Some of us by nature hold back more and are less quick to share personal thoughts and feelings. This may be because it is difficult for us to find the right words to express our feelings. Or we may have been raised in a family where parents and children did not usually talk much about their feelings or display them often. We may have learned from childhood that emotions are private and should be kept to oneself.

Some of our feelings may embarrass us, particularly if we are used to hiding what we feel. Natalie felt very scared of learning to drive but did not let anyone know. She had avoided it when all her friends learned at age sixteen, but now that she had found a better job twenty miles from home, she was forced to learn. Natalie was in quite a quandary. Her roommates kept offering to teach her. She needed to learn, but she felt too frightened. Yet she could not tell them that fear kept her from accepting their offers. But when her cat ran away and never came back, Natalie was more comfortable letting everyone know how sad she felt. In fact, Natalie's style mirrored what she had learned at home as a child, where the family showed sadness and grief openly but never talked about fear or anxiety.

Many women consider such emotions as anger, guilt, shame, jealousy, envy, and hatred as bad, and no matter how openly they share love and joy, they keep the "bad" feelings to themselves. This style makes enduring the bad feelings more painful, because we lose the chance to learn that everyone experiences them, that they are a normal part of human nature. We lose the chance to feel more connected to people who sometimes feel as we do. Instead, we feel more alone.

Rather than focusing on controlling natural feelings as if they were dangerous, we might want to think about people with whom it would be safe and comfortable to share them, and those situations in which it would be all right to let others know what we feel. We do not always want to share our feelings, nor do we always want to keep them to ourselves. Rather, we want to choose the times when we can express them comfortably and constructively.

Barbara's boss had a habit of criticizing her in front of her colleagues. She was an accountant and her boss had been doing this for several years, but Barbara, who was used to keeping things to herself and afraid the boss would criticize her even more if she complained, hid her growing anger and hurt. The last straw occurred at a

Christmas party where her boss launched into what he thought was a humorous description of her inability to keep well-organized files on her clients. Barbara knew that a party was not the place for a confrontation, but she decided then and there to talk to him on Monday morning about how bad he made her feel. On that Monday the first of several discussions took place that eventually helped her boss to realize what he had been doing, so that he could try to change.

There are times when, after we have kept our feelings to ourselves for a long period, we suddenly can hold back no longer and explode in situations in which we would rather have kept quiet. Although as we grow into adulthood, we become better able to moderate our emotions and to choose when and where and to whom we want to express them, we are not perfect. There are times when our feelings show—in our faces, through gestures, in our voices, and in our actions—when we may not expect it or want it that way.

At times like these, we may feel embarrassed and upset at having lost our temper or crying. But we should take this as a sign that some of our feelings have been bottled up too long. Instead of being ashamed or embarrassed, we should use the occurrence to help ourselves and others understand what we have been feeling and how others have affected us.

As adults, we are aiming for some regulation of expression of our emotions, some middle ground between keeping them all to ourselves and expressing everything as soon as we feel it, no matter where we are. But since no one reaches this state of perfection, all we can do is struggle with our feelings and accept our imperfections.

Some of us would like to be more able to share our feelings with people we are close to but find it difficult to come up with the right words. This may appear to be a fairly simple problem to solve, merely requiring a few key words or phrases. In reality, however, translating feelings into words is not easy. All of us have difficulty with it from time to time, but for some people it is particularly hard.

How can you find words to express the intense fury you may feel when a burglar breaks into your home and steals the few precious pieces of jewelry you had to remind you of your dead mother? How can we find words to express the joy of sex with a man we love and care about? How can we find words to express our intense love, loyalty, and commitment to the man we have been married to for three decades? The use of poetry to express intense feelings attests to the difficulty of finding everyday words that do the job.

Sharing feelings with people we are close to is one way of feeling connected to other people. Human beings are social animals. We are designed to want to be with other people and to feel unpleasantly alone and lonely when deprived of human contact. Emotional connectedness is one crucial aspect of that contact, and as imperfect as words may be, they are the medium by which we usually make and sustain our connection to others.

Flora, for example, grieved intensely for her fourteen-year-old dog when he died. She had lived alone with him all those years. They had camped and traveled together, and even her close friends and family could not fill the gap he left. But for weeks after he died, Flora kept her feelings to herself. In fact, she did not even tell many people about her loss. She did not know how to explain such intense love and grief over a dog and worried that people would not understand.

In a park one day in which she had often walked the dog, Flora met another woman she had sometimes talked to as they both walked their pets. When Beth wondered, "Why didn't you bring Ruggles with you today?" Flora admitted that the dog had died. Beth immediately stopped walking and told Flora, "How awful that must be for you," and launched into an emotional description of how hard it had been for her and her family when their previous dog died. Beth's intensity of feeling for her pet relieved Flora, who felt she could finally talk about Ruggles to someone who would understand.

Research has shown that having others with whom we can share intense feelings protects us from getting overwhelmed. When we are connected—through school, job, church, or community—to groups of people, we are less likely to be overcome by emotions that stress and crisis can generate. Scientists have found that being a member of such groups helps us solve problems and feel cared for and respected. This situation is different from talking to friends and family, because it means that we feel connected to many people at once.

Julie moved to a new city for a good job. Luckily she had some friends and family there, but after a few months she began to feel lonely and blue. She saw her two girlfriends and an elderly aunt and uncle fairly often, but somehow that contact was not enough to keep her from feeling alone. Things improved considerably when Julie joined a church group and became involved in establishing a halfway house for women who suddenly found themselves without shelter. At first, it was difficult for her to get to know people, and she felt shy and uncomfortable, but after a few months her loneliness and blues began to go away.

Sometimes we can get a lot of support from self-help groups that women form to help one another with particular problems. Laura, a single mother with a five-year-old son, decided to join a group of four women who also had children they were raising without husbands. Laura had felt guilty because her busy work schedule meant she could not spend as much time with Timmy as she thought he needed. It was quite a relief to her to learn that the four women were in the same bind, and to be able to sort out how realistic their feelings of guilt really were.

Naomi also belonged to a self-help group, but one that was directed toward a more specific goal. She was part of a group of ten women writers who met each week in each other's homes to talk over their work and the problems with editors and contracts. Since they each worked alone, they could get quite lonely, and meeting together reinforced their identities and value as writers even when editors were giving them a hard time. Sharing their doubts, fears, and anxieties diminished the unpleasant feelings. They also helped each other find solutions to problems they were facing in their work.

Psychologists and psychiatrists have begun to recognize that the strong need of women to be connected to other people, and to be interdependent with them, is a great asset. We can use this natural inclination to share and be with others to help us with our emotions and to help protect us, at least somewhat, from crisis and stress.

COPING THROUGH THINKING

In Chapter 1, we talked about the way we learn to name our feelings and the role that naming plays in how we respond to events and in how we express ourselves. The frightening ring of your doorbell early one Sunday morning evoked fearful thoughts and feelings because you interpreted the ringing as the delivery of bad news. Once you realized that flowers were being delivered, you gave a happier and more pleasant meaning to the initially frightening situation, and you no longer felt scared and anxious.

Some psychiatrists and psychologists believe that the meaning we give to things that happen to us has an enormous impact on how we feel. They have found that one reason people have unpleasant feelings is that they misinterpret events in their lives or misunderstand people's response to them.

Aaron Beck, M.D., has pioneered this "cognitive" approach to dealing with emotions. He believes that our thoughts create our emotions, and that we may handle our emotions better by learning to think differently. Monica, a new teacher, felt very anxious about talking in front of her classes. Each time the hour for a lecture approached, she felt knots in her stomach, her legs began to shake, and her usually articulate speech deteriorated into mumbling. Things got so bad that the principal told her she would have to leave at the end of the semester unless she could teach more effectively.

The cognitive psychotherapy that Dr. Beck developed is usually short-term. After ten weeks of counseling, Monica was able to lecture sensibly and informatively to her classes. Even some of her anxiety—the shakiness and stomach knots—had diminished quite a bit.

What was behind Monica's fear that could be changed in such a relatively brief time? Her cognitive therapist focused on what it meant to Monica to be a teacher. Monica saw her job as providing information to classes of forty students who might ask questions in return. To Monica, teaching meant knowing everything the students might want to know. She thought that unless she had complete knowledge of a subject before she faced a class, she would be inadequate and look stupid if she did not know the answer to every possible question.

Monica's thoughts about what it meant to be a teacher were not realistic and appeared to be the cause of the extreme anxiety she experienced at work. Her psychotherapist helped her change her ideas about what it meant to be a good teacher, and as her thoughts became more realistic, her anxiety diminished.

How often do we give unrealistic or distorted meanings to the things that happen or to the way people react to us? How often do we feel blue because a close friend has not called in many weeks, without checking to find out her explanation? How often do we automatically assume, instead, that she no longer likes us or wants to be our friend?

The first step in coping through thinking takes place when we react to people or events with unpleasant and puzzling emotions. At this time, we will want to observe our thoughts about those people and events, and pay attention to the thoughts that come before and accompany our feelings. We may be surprised at what we find.

Cornelia had exactly this experience when she attended Christmas dinner at the home of a family she had never met. Having just moved far away from her own large family, she felt fortunate to have received an invitation so soon from the Merricks, whom her parents had known for several years. Despite her initial feelings of happiness, Cornelia began to feel blue and uncomfortable soon after she arrived at the Merricks' home. After dinner, she hid in an upstairs bathroom to try to stop crying and become more presentable to this generous family. She could not understand why she was feeling this bad.

Several months later, while visiting her own family for the first time since she moved, it suddenly occurred to Cornelia how much the Merricks had reminded her of them. Being at the Merricks', she realized, meant that she was far away from where she really wanted to be on that special holiday. That meaning, which took months for her to become aware of, seemed to be the cause of her inexplicable blues on Christmas.

We can use the "coping through thinking" technique to help us handle many troublesome and puzzling emotions, because all our emotions are accompanied by thoughts. Sometimes it is important not only to observe what we think but also to check out the evidence for our beliefs. Do our beliefs really match what we know about ourselves and others? We have pointed out in Chapter 2 that when we feel guilty we usually think we have done something wrong and have failed ourselves or others in some way. We may tend to pay more attention to our bad feelings than to the thoughts that come with them. But careful observance of those thoughts may show us that they are askew. Once we figure that out, we will be more able to deal realistically with our guilty feelings, which may diminish.

Linda felt guilty for several years because she had not completed college, as her parents had wanted. She worked at a job that she liked, but she could never enjoy it fully because of nagging feelings that she should really be in college. Visiting her parents stirred up her guilt even more, so she avoided them, and this made her feel even worse.

Linda used to be fairly content and happy, but she had not felt really good about herself since she dropped out of college. She had never talked to anyone about these feelings until she accidentally met a classmate with whom she had roomed during her two years in college. Corinne had finished her degree but had not been able to find a job, and while she did not feel guilty, she was far less happy than Linda.

This surprising discovery forced Linda to do some hard thinking about her own feelings. She realized that she had equated dropping out of college with failing her parents, and that failing her parents meant to her that she was a "bad person." This awareness did not come overnight, it developed gradually, until Linda was shocked to find that she had given such a negative meaning to a decision she had made carefully and with the advice of others, including her parents. Her discovery about her sweeping interpretation of what it meant to drop out of college hit her hard, but it helped her ease some of the guilt she had felt for so long.

Using our thoughts to handle our feelings requires that we pay attention to what we are thinking. This can be difficult when we are very upset or overwhelmed by our feelings. At these times, we may need to talk our thoughts out with a friend or family member so that he or she can help us figure out which of our thoughts led to our unpleasant emotions.

Coping through thinking is not for everybody or for every situation. Sometimes our emotions are so intense and so confused and out of control that we may want to seek professional help. But at times in our everyday lives, most of us have unrealistic, distorted, or negative thoughts that can lead to bad feelings. If we become adept at figuring out what these thoughts are, we can help ourselves to feel better.

WHEN YOU CANNOT HANDLE YOUR FEELINGS: ASKING FOR HELP

There may be times in our lives when many stressful or difficult things happen at once and shake our usual emotional balance. Michelle was happily single, and comfortable sharing her emotions with friends or keeping them to herself, depending on the situation. But when unpleasant things began to happen in her life, she lost her even keel and felt panicky and anxious more and more often.

In March, Michelle took a new job that she had wanted badly and that was difficult for her from the very first day. By April, she had already had several disagreements with her supervisor, and relations between the two were deteriorating. In May, another person for whom she also did some work suggested that Michelle leave his division, but she insisted that things would get better and resolved to remain. She was working seventy hours a week in order to meet all the demands of her new job. By summer, Michelle, feeling exhausted and overwhelmed, broke up with her boyfriend, for whom she cared very much. She spent much of August crying, and asked her supervisor if she could work fewer hours for a while because she felt too overwhelmed but he refused her request, and Michelle finally had to quit.

Michelle missed the close circle of friends she had made at her new job and spent a lot of time at home alone, upset, and not knowing what to do. She had little energy and began to stay in bed during the day. She went out less and less frequently because going out of the house made her anxious. Michelle's usual way of handling her emotions was not working. She was so overwhelmed by anxiety, anger, and depression that she could not sort out the feelings enough even to talk to friends.

One friend, worried about how much time Michelle spent in bed, finally suggested she talk to a psychiatrist who might be able to help her understand why she felt so upset and help her do something about it. The psychiatrist felt that she needed medication to diminish her depression. This helped a bit, but Michelle also continued weekly visits for a year to talk about the job and supervisor and boyfriend who had upset her so much in the first place. At times, the counseling itself upset her, because it reminded her of things she would rather forget, but little by little she began to feel better.

Michelle's reaction is more serious than most of us will experience during our lives, although we may have friends or relatives who respond as she did to intense stress. We do not necessarily require psychotherapy or medication for those times when we feel overwhelmed by our emotions and find our usual methods of coping

failing to work. But for some of us, talking to a professional trained to help people with their feelings may be
helpful, even if things are not as bad as they were for
Michelle.

Sometimes we may want to talk with a person who is
outside our usual circle of friends and may choose a
psychologist or a minister, who might be more objective
than the friends and relatives who are intimately involved in our lives. Both ministers and psychotherapists
are bound by a code of confidentiality, so that whatever
we tell them remains private.

After three years of marriage, Susan realized she was
too unhappy to stay with her husband. She felt ashamed
and guilty that she had not worked hard enough to make
things better, and she did not want to share her sadness
and feelings of failure with friends or family. She approached her minister, with whom she had spoken only
briefly before, and requested a meeting.

They talked over the problems Susan had experienced
in her marriage and how bad she felt that things had not
gone better. It was helpful when the minister agreed that
her marital problems sounded quite serious and upsetting—Susan's husband had become an alcoholic and had
tried to beat her several times—and let Susan know that
she had done a lot more than she was aware of to make
the marriage work. Susan and the minister met a dozen
times until she felt able to tell her husband, her family,
and her friends that things were not working out and she
planned to separate from him. Her decision shocked her
husband, and he agreed to begin an Alcoholics Anony-
mous program, which until then he had refused to do.

It can be difficult to admit that our usual ways of
dealing with emotions are not working and that we need
professional help to get things back in order. We may feel
that it is weak to seek the help of a psychotherapist or
pastoral counselor to handle what we have usually han-

dled well ourselves. But there are times when stress may be severe, when we may find ourselves in new and difficult situations, when we want a fresh perspective on how things are going, or when we simply do not understand why we feel as bad or as upset as we do. At these times, we may want to seek professional help, particularly if the troubles continue despite our efforts to resolve them.

Just as sharing our emotions with close friends and relatives can bring relief and broadened perspective, so talking with a trained professional about our feelings and about difficult events in our lives can provide new understanding of what we are feeling and why. These are experiences we can build on and grow from.

CHAPTER 4

Our Emotions Affect
Those Around Us

OUR EMOTIONS ARE A UNIQUE PART OF US

People have different temperaments. Some of us actually experience more intense emotions than others. We all probably know people whom we consider particularly "emotional" because we have noticed that they feel more, or express more emotions, when reacting to people and events.

Janice stood out in her family as more emotional than her three brothers and sisters. She had been like that from childhood, always getting the most excited when the family planned a trip to the circus or the theater. She also seemed to feel sad more often than the others, crying for days after the family's dog died, when everyone else calmed down much sooner.

Psychologists studying infants have observed differences in temperament almost immediately after birth. Some infants move around more, seem more restless and irritable, and cry more frequently than others who appear to be consistently calmer and more content. This conclusion should not surprise mothers with two or more children who notice differences in their infants' sleeping and eating habits, in how irritable they become when wet or hungry, in how much they cry, and even in how much they smile and like to be cuddled. Psychologists believe that many of these differences are inborn.

Each of us, then, starts out life with varying emotional equipment, which means that people around us respond uniquely to how we express ourselves and act. Parents react to a calm baby who smiles frequently differently from the way they react to a baby who cries a lot and seems more irritable when uncomfortable. Our parents' response to us as infants can modify our emotional equipment somewhat, either intensifying it or diminishing it.

Experiences as we grow up also modify what we are born with. As we have already mentioned, girls are encouraged to feel and express certain emotions (fear, for example), whereas boys are encouraged to keep such feelings more to themselves but to express other feelings, such as anger and defiance, more readily. A succession of experiences with parents, friends, and teachers, added to the temperament with which we were born, combine to make us unique in how much emotion we feel, in how we handle our feelings, and in whether we share them with others.

Differences in people's temperaments and emotionality can make relationships difficult and frustrating, but also a lot more interesting. Life would be pretty dull if we all felt exactly the same range of feelings—which may be one reason we often choose friends and partners who are the emotional opposites of ourselves.

Alice and Audrey, two middle-aged sisters who lived together, often joked that Alice took care of the thinking for both of them and that Audrey took care of the feeling. It wasn't that Audrey couldn't think; in fact, she was a successful computer programmer. And it wasn't that Alice couldn't feel, although she usually kept her emotions to herself. Alice and Audrey got along very well because they complemented each other's capacities. Audrey automatically responded to people and events emotionally, while Alice responded more by thinking things over.

Each of us is endowed with unique emotional capacities that we can learn to live with and accept. Rebecca did not understand this until she separated from her husband. Bill had always felt intensely about things and talked openly about feeling sad, happy, joyful, and depressed. He laughed a lot and cried a lot. Rebecca, on the other hand, felt little emotion and could not understand Bill's intense feelings. In fact, he did not like her style either and tried to convince her, early in their four-year marriage, that she should try to become more emotional like him. It was only after they separated that Rebecca realized she liked herself the way she was and that it was all right to be less intense and to hold back her feelings. In fact, she decided that her husband, with his insistence on being emotional, probably overdid it.

Not only do individuals vary in the ways they handle and express emotion, but families and cultures differ too. For example, studies of Japanese newborns have shown that, compared to American infants, the Japanese are much calmer, less irritable, and less active when first born. Inborn differences such as these interact with the way young children are raised and with their life experiences in growing up, producing adults with a great range of emotional intensity and styles.

Some families express and share emotions more frequently and more openly than others. We probably all know families where everything is everybody's business, and other families where members not only keep feelings to themselves but are actually secretive about their emotional lives. Many families are at neither extreme, but rather share some emotions at certain times, frequently considering some feelings more acceptable to share than others.

Anita's family always ate their evening meal together and used that time to share the events of the day and the feelings they evoked. Mealtime in the Brockton household was noisy and talkative, with everyone wanting to tell his or her story and not always willing to wait for a turn. Things always seemed to work out by the end of the hour, though, because Anita and her husband made sure all three children had some time to talk and a chance to respond and share their feelings too.

The Brocktons reserved mealtime for this special sharing among family members, but they did not expect it to go on at other times. When their eight-year-old son Larry came home from school, eager to share the praise he had won from a teacher, his mother nonchalantly asked him to "wait for dinner so everyone can hear about it at once."

Although there is no ideal way to share emotions in family life, and no ideal family that does a perfect job, counselors who work with families believe that at least some emotional expression is important. Like a woman who lets all her feelings accumulate inside until she feels bad enough to share them or becomes overwhelmed by them or even explodes, the family that does not share feelings with each other may not work as well together as a unit. In fact, they may not be much of a unit at all.

In some families, sisters and brothers share their feelings with each other and provide support during crises that they would rather not discuss with their parents. Diane and Marvin, two teenagers, found that they could help each other when one faced a problem with the opposite sex. They relied on each other for advice and provided a shoulder to cry on when things did not work out. Teenagers sometimes feel that parents don't understand their problems, so this brother and sister had developed a good substitute arrangement.

People who are raised in varying types of families and people with different temperaments may find it difficult to understand each other. While some of us seek friends, lovers, and husbands who differ from us in enough ways to make the relationship interesting and alive, we can go too far and become involved with a man who is so much our opposite emotionally that the relationship becomes very rocky.

Each of us is born with unique emotional equipment which is shaped and modified as we grow up and learn to understand our feelings better and find new ways to express them. It is ironic that in order to connect emotionally with other people and to be able to share our feelings over long periods of time, we must often make changes in the style of expressing our emotions that we have spent years developing. Jennifer found herself in love with a man who openly and intensely expressed his feelings. She was not used to this, having come from a family where feelings were more subdued and men did not cry. Before meeting Doug, Jennifer herself had finally become able to talk about her feelings comfortably, but Doug's openness was a big surprise. At thirty, Jennifer found herself struggling once again with her style of emotional expression and learning to accept her new partner's very different manner.

Emotional development continues throughout our lives. Experiences during our childhood years do not solely determine the kind of adults we grow into. Our experiences as older children, as teenagers, and as young adults also shape our emotional style. As we grow older, we learn from each other new ways of handling feelings, and sometimes we even learn to feel in ways that we could not before. An experience in a special relationship (with a close friend or husband or psychotherapist, for instance) can modify the emotional styles we grew up with and may have felt comfortable—or uncomfortable—with for years.

This was true for Denise, who was used to expressing her anger openly. She screamed at close friends and at her husband when she was angry, and ten minutes later her intense feelings dissolved and she was ready to talk again as if nothing had happened. This style had always puzzled her friends, who wondered how she could be so angry that she yelled at them, yet felt friendly again so quickly.

While her friends had accepted Denise's habit, her husband could not. Her quick change of mood from anger to warmth and friendliness confused him, and he particularly did not like to be yelled at. Once she got angry and yelled, he got angry too, but his anger lasted much longer, so he could not respond to her warmth ten minutes later. With her husband so upset about a style of emotional expression that Denise had used for years, she felt forced to reexamine its effects on other people and began to try to talk when she became angry, instead of raising her voice.

 Now that people are living longer, they are more likely to become involved in a larger number of close relationships and may have to compromise, even as senior citizens, in the way they live emotionally with other people. This is not an easy task, but it is possible, because people have the capacity for change and growth throughout their lifetimes.

EMOTIONS AFFECT RELATIONSHIPS

Emotions make us feel more vulnerable, especially when we let other people know what we are feeling. Once we let down the barrier that protects us from other people, it is easier to feel hurt when they reject us, appear uninterested in our feelings, or criticize us. But even aside from the added vulnerability we experience when we share our emotions, just being aware of our feelings can make us feel more open to hurt and rejection.

This vulnerability comes from the feeling that we cannot control our emotions in the same way we may think we can control our thoughts. Emotions can be scary, because once we feel them we do not know exactly where they will lead. Our thoughts, on the other hand, rarely feel out of control. Although we may at times feel a bit scatterbrained and forget what we set out to say or do, most of us do not find our thoughts frightening, and we are often able to communicate them comfortably to other people.

But if we feel angry or sad, who knows where it will lead? If we begin to tell a friend about our sadness, will we start crying and be unable to quiet down? What will our friend think? Will she believe that we are overestimating the seriousness of our situation, that we are foolish to feel so upset? Will she not like our crying and ask us to stop?

Keeping the sadness inside may make us feel just as vulnerable. Once we feel sad, the usual slights and inconveniences of everyday life may become more powerful. At seventeen, Judy felt very sad when her closest brother married and moved to another city. She felt so rejected and so bad about herself that it hurt when a cabdriver acted insolently, when the mail carrier refused to redeliver a certified letter, when a friend said she could not meet for dinner on a certain evening. Unpleasant feelings such as sadness, depression, envy, and anger can make the ordinary aspects of our lives seem suddenly more painful.

But it is not just the unpleasant emotions that make us feel more vulnerable. When we love and care about another person, we are also vulnerable to feelings of rejection or hurt. Loving another person—be it parent, child, husband, or friend—is a heavy investment, and a frightening one, because we may wonder if our love will be reciprocated and respected. Love also makes us vulnerable, because we could lose the people we love or they themselves could become hurt, wounding us in the process.

Our vulnerability when we feel emotional also has positive aspects to it. What we experience as vulnerability may be viewed by others as a special sensitivity and an asset. Sensitivity is the strong side of vulnerability. This capacity offers us a chance to get to know ourselves better, to understand more about what goes on inside us and how we react to various situations and people.

When Lori realized how much she loved her parents, she began to look back at how they had raised her and her brother. Lori made this discovery when she was just thirteen and her father suffered a serious heart attack. She felt frightened and worried about what might happen to him, and she missed him more than she ever expected during the weeks he spent in the hospital. Her love for her father made her vulnerable to fear and anxiety over his well-being and over the possibility of losing him. But out of this vulnerability, Lori discovered how much she cared about him and learned more about her own feelings.

Lori's experience with her father's illness is one way that emotions bring people closer together. We can connect with other people in several ways: through talking, through physical touch, through eye contact, through facial expression and body language, and through sharing emotions. In fact, human beings have developed rituals for sharing times of deep emotion. At funerals and weddings, and on holidays, we get together to share our feelings of loss or joy or love for God.

Rituals bring together people who feel emotionally connected and involved in one another's lives. They connect us further to people we care about by revitalizing relationships as emotions are shared. But this is work that also occurs in our everyday lives. How often has it happened that you felt distant from a person whom you thought you did not know well, until the two of you shared the same emotional experience which brought you closer together?

Elena worked in the same office for almost a year with three other women whom she barely knew. They all worked hard on their own projects and got along fine, but they socialized little and knew little about one another's private lives. Then there was a serious fire in the building on a morning when all four women were busy at their desks. As the alarms went off, they pooled what they knew about procedure in such situations and got out quickly from their seventh-floor office by rushing down the nearest stairwell.

They had not panicked, and by the time they got to the ground floor and realized just how serious the fire was, they all felt very frightened. For several hours, as people asked them, they recounted how they had escaped and felt lucky that they had all worked together so efficiently. When they returned to work a few days later, the atmosphere in the office had changed. The four women talked again about the fire and about their reactions, and week by week they became closer to one another, sharing for the first time information about their personal lives.

It does not always take an emotional crisis or a shared emotional experience for people to feel more connected by sharing feelings. Sometimes we can simply start to talk to a friend about our children and end up involved in a discussion of how we feel when our children act angrily toward us. Anne and Darlene had separately worried about how angry their children could become when their mothers refused to allow them to play at homework time. They both felt relieved when they discovered that each had the same experiences and the same fears.

Anne felt closer to Darlene after this conversation, so she shared yet another worry that had bothered her for a long time, something she felt ashamed about. Her eighteen-year-old brother—five years younger than she— kept telling her that he hated her, and this upset Anne greatly. Darlene had not experienced such a situation with her own brother, but the two women talked about it and decided it probably was not so terrible after all, because teenagers often feel confused about their feelings and Steven probably felt envious of Anne's independence. This sharing helped both women feel better, and it brought them closer together.

This kind of emotional sharing brings people closer together over the many years that a relationship endures. This is one reason we are often more comfortable with people we have known for a long time. We have shared so much of our emotional selves with each other that we are no longer as separate as we were when we first started out, and this connectedness gives us support and comfort as we face the inevitable stresses of everyday life.

Just as emotions can bring people together, they can also pull people apart. Emotions, particularly intense ones, can be frightening, and people close to someone in the midst of deep despair or severe anger or hatred may become scared and want to get away. And if two people feel intensely about something, but in opposite directions, so that they disagree, conflict and argument may result.

Lisa found out that strong emotions can scare people off shortly after her father, Gerald, died. Not only had she been her father's favorite child, but he had provided well for their family. After his death, Lisa felt doubly deprived of the emotional closeness and the comfortable material life she had been used to. Now the family had to worry about money and could not spend freely as in the past.

Lisa changed from a happy and well-liked teenager to a jealous and self-pitying one. She envied everything her friends had, particularly their fathers, and felt sorry for herself because her own father had died. She withdrew from her friends and began to fail at school.

Lisa's emotions caused conflict with her friends and worry in her family. Her mother and sister and brother had also been close to Gerald, but they were more able to mourn and accept his death and continue with their lives. Finally, Lisa's mother went to see a psychologist to talk about Lisa's troubles, and eventually encouraged her reluctant daughter to accompany her. The psychologist helped Lisa accept her anger at her father for his unexpected and premature death. He made her more comfortable with her deprivation by explaining that it is common for people to feel angry and cheated by the death of those they love. After a few months of counseling, Lisa was able to talk about her loss and her sadness, and she became less withdrawn. But it took over a year for her to feel well enough to improve her grades.

Emotions affect relationships in unpredictable ways, because we cannot force ourselves to feel as others might like us to, nor can we control the course of our emotional lives. A full emotional life enriches the relationships we enter into and connects us more firmly with people we are close to.

LIVING WITH THE EMOTIONS OF OTHERS

One key to living more comfortably with those around us is to accept their fallibility as well as our own. None of us have perfect emotions which we express only at the correct moments. Feelings do not always wait for the most opportune time for expression, and the emotional needs and concerns of those we live with may inconvenience us at various times.

Wendy felt very put out by the constant grieving of her father-in-law for his wife, who had died months earlier. Theodore had gone to live with his son and Wendy soon after his wife's death, but could not seem to recover, and either stayed in his room alone or talked incessantly about how differently Wendy ran her home from his late—and "more perfect"—wife. It took eight months for Theodore to begin to get out of the house again and see friends and adjust to his wife's death. Wendy had been patient throughout his long period of mourning, and she felt glad about this now that the two could begin to enjoy each other's company as they had done before.

Just as the people we love, live with, and work with are imperfect in other ways, they are also imperfect when it comes to handling and expressing their feelings. If we have accepted our own fallibility and imperfections, it will make it easier to accept those of others. But if we are overly critical of ourselves, it is likely that we will be too critical of other people as well.

Self-acceptance is difficult, particularly when it requires accepting feelings in ourselves that we find shameful, unpleasant, or painful. Many of us have grown up to believe that feelings of anger or envy or hate are bad, and that "good people" do not experience them. In fact, we all endure these feelings from time to time. They are normal aspects of human emotional life. So when we encounter them in others, we will want to try to be accepting of them, understanding that having these feelings does not make people bad.

Most of us have struggled in our marriages and in our relationships with parents to accept their imperfections. Sometimes we can manage this, and the relationship goes on to develop and grow more smoothly. But when we cannot accept the imperfections of a husband's or a parent's emotional life, the relationship can founder and become unhappy and unsatisfying.

Lenore, now thirty-three, had such a problem with her mother almost since she was a child. She and her mother had very different temperaments, and Lenore's restlessness and openness conflicted with her mother's contentment and reserve. Throughout the years of growing up, mother and daughter fought often, never able to accept the other's style but each wishing they had a more perfect companion. Unable to work out a compromise between their different temperaments and their different beliefs about how emotions should be handled, Lenore and her mother became even more distant once the daughter grew up and left home.

There are times in our lives when we feel unable to accept particular imperfections in others and will sometimes become emotionally distant from them because of this. This is a high price to pay for our inability to accept the imperfections that are part of human nature.

At other times, we may choose to help people we care about with their feelings rather than move away from them. This is not an easy job either, because few of us have our own emotions in such perfect order that we can see clearly the kind of help a husband or parent or friend might need.

Helen wanted to help her best friend, Nanette, get over the death of her sister, with whom she had been very close. Nanette grieved intensely when her sister died, and Helen simply did not know what to do to comfort her friend. Part of Helen's dilemma grew out of her own sister's death several months earlier. Helen and her sister had been quite distant, and she had always felt envious of Nanette's closeness with her own sister This made it very difficult for Helen to be comforting at such a rough period in Nanette's life.

There are times in our lives when we are not able to give the comfort or support we would like to offer to people in emotional difficulty. Sometimes we have little to give because we ourselves are under stress and experiencing our own emotional problems.

At other times, we can be helpful to parents, husband, or close friends, whose emotions have overwhelmed them. Sometimes all people need is a sympathetic ear, because talking about their feelings can be a great relief and set them back on an even keel. During other periods, listening is not quite enough, because our friend's or husband's or parent's emotions may be so tangled and painful that we need to talk to them a lot about their feelings.

Celia discovered this was the situation with Martin when he was fired from his job for failing to follow company regulations. It was the third time in five years of marriage that this had happened, so Martin felt not only wounded by this last rejection but also anxious and fearful about what it said about his ability to work with people. He also worried about ending up like his father, who had never been able to keep a job or support their family adequately. Martin felt that once again he had let Celia and his two-year-old twin sons down.

Celia wanted to help Martin cope with this complicated situation that had stirred up earlier losses and fears about reliving his father's life. But Martin became so depressed that he required more than a sympathetic ear to feel better. Celia did not really understand what made it so difficult for her husband to follow company regulations, but she hoped she could at least show him how different he was from his own father, and comfort him by helping him feel less guilty and worried about his own family.

The two of them did lots of talking and sharing during the few weeks after Martin lost his job, a sharing that brought them closer together emotionally. But Martin still felt he had problems to work through that talking to Celia could not solve, and the two of them decided that he would see a counselor to try to understand his difficulties better.

Sometimes the best help we can offer a loved one who is dealing with difficult emotions is the suggestion that they seek professional help. Although we may not like to acknowledge that a sympathetic ear and a heavy dose of comfort are not enough, there are times when a person needs the perspective and guidance of a trained outside listener.

Asking for help of any kind is difficult for many people, whether it is help from a relative or friend or help from a professional counselor or psychotherapist. People sometimes feel that requiring help for emotional difficulties is a sign of weakness, and they will keep their troubles to themselves and struggle with them alone longer than is necessary. Suggesting outside help in these situations requires that we be tactful and diplomatic about the problems we see.

Celia knew how hard it was for her husband to admit defeat a third time, and that he would consider asking for help—even from her—a sign of failure and weakness. She was very careful not to ask him much about the situation at work but to let him tell her the story as he wanted to tell it. She was there to listen and be supportive, but not to grill him about the rules he broke or his bosses' rejection. Even when it came to the decision to seek professional counseling, she let him bring it up first, rather than tactlessly suggesting that after losing three jobs it was obviously what he needed. An approach like that would probably have upset and scared Martin even more.

There are times when we cannot help people who are having emotional difficulty, and when we need instead to protect ourselves from being too affected by their troubles. This is a decision we might want to make carefully if we are close to the person in trouble and feel we cannot offer any help. Our action can be taken as a hurtful rejection by someone who is already experiencing more than usual stress, so we want to handle such a situation as gently as possible.

We all have imperfect lives, and we all have our own troubles. Few of us are problem free. Yet we often feel capable of helping others with the emotional ups and downs of their lives, especially those close to us. In fact, emotional support can be an expected part of certain relationships: husband and wife, parent and child, brother and sister, and close friendships. In deciding that we must protect ourselves from someone's emotional upheaval, it is important to distinguish between these kinds of relationships and those that are not as close.

We cannot be supportive and comforting to everyone who becomes emotionally upset. Women, in particular, often seem to feel responsible for helping people they know who are overwhelmed by their emotions. Traditionally, women are the ones who are supposed to provide the nurturance and emotional support in a relationship, and sometimes we make too many sacrifices ourselves to fill this expectation.

As a result, we may want to choose carefully those people whom we nurture and comfort when they get into emotional trouble. There are people in our lives to whom we are strongly committed, and we may want to devote most of our energy to them.

Lois was an exceptionally giving woman who felt constantly drawn to people in distress. She felt needed by them and tried hard to give them the emotional support they required. Lois was known among her friends as the most sympathetic ear and the person to go to if things got rough. This worked fine for everyone, until Lois became engaged to marry. She continued to see her friends, but she had less time to listen to their problems.

Around the time of Lois' wedding, one friend separated from her husband and leaned heavily on Lois for comfort and support. She called Lois on the phone at least once a day and expected to see her several times a week. Lois did not want to hurt Angela's feelings, but with her new commitment to a partner and with her wedding approaching, she did not feel able to handle Angela's troubles. Lois found it particularly difficult because Angela wanted to discuss leaving her husband just when Lois herself was planning for her own married life. Angela's troubles made Lois anxious, and she wanted to escape.

Finally, Lois felt she must stop seeing Angela until her friend got her feelings more under control. Lois decided that the least hurtful way to do this was to let Angela know how nervous and upset she was about her own upcoming wedding, rather than blame Angela's neediness for making it impossible to be with her.

It is very difficult to refuse to help people when they need something from us emotionally. We may feel selfish and guilty when we do what Lois did to protect herself from getting overwhelmed at a stressful time in her life.

Sometimes we may be able to protect ourselves emotionally by putting more distance between ourselves and another person, but continuing to see them. Frances managed this with her sister, who brought to her all the troubles she was having with her son. When Frances felt she could no longer be helpful to her sister, having listened to her complaints and given unheeded advice for so long, she gently told her they should talk about other things. In fact, they finally agreed not to discuss Robbie at all when they got together, preserving their relationship in a comfortable way.

Some of us are better than others at "tuning out" other people's emotions when we feel scared or overwhelmed by them. In this way, we can spend time with a friend or relative but not become overly involved with their trou-bles. Those of us who are not so adept at this sometimes need to distance ourselves physically when we feel that others are demanding more than we can give at the moment.

Although this may make us feel ashamed and guilty, we are really just accepting our limitations as human beings. We are not perfect and cannot give emotionally to everyone all the time. Sometimes we need to take care of ourselves or of those to whom we have more serious commitments. It is important to be realistic about our limitations as emotional care-givers and accept ourselves as we are.

CHAPTER 5

What About Men?

AS BOYS, MEN ARE OFTEN TAUGHT NOT TO EXPRESS THEIR FEELINGS

Although things are gradually changing, it is still common practice to raise girls and boys to handle their feelings differently. We expect girls to be emotional and to express their feelings. As a result, we do not discourage them from crying or feeling sad or upset when they fall and cut themselves or when a friend rejects them. Little boys, on the other hand, are supposed to keep a "stiff upper lip" and learn that they should hide their hurt feelings in order to act like a man. Acting like a man usually includes expressing other kinds of feelings such as anger and defiance.

Not only do we often encourage girls to handle their emotions differently from boys, but when children watch their parents they notice that their mothers cry and act emotionally, whereas their fathers seem tougher, more "rational," and more in control of their weaker sides. Girls will try to behave more like their mothers, boys more like their fathers.

Psychologists have found that in our society training to

be men and women begins immediately after birth. Parents react differently to a newborn boy than to a newborn girl. They seem to smile more at baby girls than at baby boys. They also seem to cuddle infant girls more frequently, and in fact continue throughout childhood to be more affectionate toward their girls than their boys.

In addition, psychologists have found that there are more restrictions placed on emotional expression on the part of boys than on the part of girls. We call girls who act more masculine "tomboys," and while we may not favor their behavior, parents are usually not ashamed that their daughters are behaving a bit like little boys. They often assume, in fact, that they will grow out of it.

Boys who behave like girls have a more serious problem in American society. Rodney, a funny and happy four-year-old, liked playing with his sister's dolls and talked about someday having his own to take care of. Rodney did not like to play with boys as much, because he "didn't enjoy their games," and he cried when they hurt his feelings by calling him "sissy." Rodney's parents were worried about this. His mother had been a tomboy herself, and everyone had thought it was cute and would eventually pass. But somehow it frightened her more when a boy took on some feminine traits than when a girl took on masculine traits.

According to Jean Baker Miller, the psychiatrist who has studied female psychology, these differences in our attitudes toward tomboys and sissies come from differences in status between men and women. Since being a man endows higher status in our culture, it is not so bad for a girl to act a bit like a boy. But women in our society have lower status than men, so permitting a boy to act like a girl, in any way, deprives him of some of his special privilege.

Because of these attitudes and because of the expectations we have of how boys and girls should behave, we end up as adults with different kinds of emotional lives. In general, women are used to feeling sadness, joy, and love, and they are used to expressing these feelings. But men may have difficulty expressing these emotions and sometimes do not even feel them. They are more able to express and act on anger, however, and to appear less vulnerable to feelings of helplessness and dependence on others.

This difference can make relationships between men and women rocky and unsatisfying unless there is some compromise that gives each partner more of what he or she needs emotionally. Brad and Dorothy experienced exactly this conflict during the first eight years of their marriage, and finally separated to try to understand better how they could give what each seemed to need. Dorothy complained that Brad could never understand her feelings, or help her when she cried or felt upset. She also felt that in eight years of marriage Brad had not let her get to know him, because he never talked about his feelings or let her know what was going on inside him. They spent a year with a marriage counselor to try to develop a more comfortable marriage.

It is important to remember that there is a wide range of differences among men and women in their capacity to feel intensely and to express those feelings. The way we raise our children merely makes it more likely that women will turn out to be in many ways more emotional than men.

Of course, these generalizations are not true for all men and women. Frieda was a reserved woman married to a volatile man, and they fought constantly over what he was feeling at a particular time. Frieda and Barry were actually quite happy together, but no one in her family could understand their style of working things out.

LIVING WITH A MAN
LESS EMOTIONAL THAN YOU

Women who marry while very young are sometimes unprepared for the emotional differences between men and women and become unhappy with their marriages. Today more and more women are taking on what used to be men's roles in the world of work outside the home. Women have become business owners, doctors, lawyers, police officers, and firefighters. At the same time, they have also retained their personal emotional lives.

Some women expect the same dual approach from men. They expect that if they can live in and manage both the world of men (work) and the world of women (emotional connectedness), men too should take on some more feminine ways. They may expect men to do some of the work at home, and some of the child-rearing, and they may also expect men to become more feeling and to express these feelings more readily.

These expectations are difficult for men to meet, even though some of them may want to. Think of how hard it must be to be taught since infancy not to cry, and at thirty-five to find that your wife wants a more emotional husband. Attitudes and styles such as this cannot change overnight. In fact, they are likely to change only if we raise future generations differently.

As a result, many women find themselves living with men who are not in touch with many of their emotions and are less willing and less able to share their emotional selves, except perhaps through sexuality. The task for women is to find ways to cope with the differences.

Many women have learned to turn to women friends for emotional sharing and support. The ability to do this is one of the strengths of women which has been overlooked and therefore not valued enough. It is not realistic to expect any one relationship to give you all you need. In fact, that expectation can place a great burden on a marriage, no matter how good the marriage may be.

Tina married at thirty and already had three or four close friends with whom she had been sharing her life for the past ten years. When she married, she did not expect her husband to take the place of these women and continued to see them and talk to them regularly. This was fine with her husband, Gordon, because he too had developed a group of friends with whom he enjoyed fishing on weekends. The marriage worked well because the couple was realistic about what they could give each other and what they could not. Gordon did not like talking to Tina about her upsets with her mother, and Tina had absolutely no interest in fishing.

Sometimes a woman may feel so deprived because of her husband's rational and unemotional approach to life, and so unconnected to him emotionally, that even close women friends and family cannot make up the difference. It can help, at these times, to get counseling from a minister or a psychologist trained to work specifically with couples or families. This can help you get a broader perspective on your marriage, its good points and its bad points, and aid in your decision about what to do.

Edith took this route when she spoke briefly to her minister one Sunday morning. For several months afterward, she met with him about how deprived she was feeling, but she also talked about her enduring love for her husband and about all the good points she admired in him. She had been feeling so deprived that she had forgotten how happy he made her in other ways. As talking with the minister reminded her of that, she realized that she was not ready to give up the marriage and decided to find out if her husband would be willing to meet with a marriage counselor to see if they could make their marriage a better one.

We all know that life requires compromises and offers disappointments for which we may be unprepared. In fact, all marriages and all relationships are imperfect, just as all human beings are imperfect. There is no perfect husband, and marriage is a set of trade-offs between expectations, needs, and wants that have different priorities and importance for us. Once involved in a marriage, we sometimes forget this, and need others to remind us of how imperfect we all are.

THINGS ARE CHANGING FOR MEN TODAY

Today it is difficult to write about relationships between men and women and about men's emotional lives because things are changing so rapidly. More and more often, men and women are sharing roles flexibly rather than adhering to more traditional divisions of labor where men worked outside the home and women worked inside.

These changes will inevitably produce differences in the way men handle and express their emotions. When men worked out of the home every day, around people who were not close friends or relatives, they usually did not openly share their feelings. But a man who starts to stay home more often and take care of the children— even just on weekends—will begin to become more aware of his feelings. In many jobs, feelings have little place, but when raising children they are important.

Gene discovered this when his wife went back to work part-time as a nurse. Two days a week she worked from three to eleven and Gene came home from work early to take care of six-month-old Jamie and three-year-old Eva. His wife had been eager to return to the profession she left when Eva was born, and Gene thought her working again was a fine idea. He took the razzing of co-workers as part of the game, but secretly looked forward to "being all alone with my kids."

Gene had never experienced intense emotions, nor was he the type to express his feelings much, and Lorraine, his wife, had gotten used to his quiet style. When she felt upset about something, she talked to her mother or sister about it, because discussing feelings with her husband, she joked, was like pulling teeth. But after three months of taking care of the children just two days a week, Gene began to change noticeably. All Gene wanted to do was to talk about the two children. He waited up for Lorraine when she came home close to midnight, eager to tell her the youngsters' latest exploits. And he talked about how they made him feel: how he felt angry and then sad when he admonished Eva for grabbing a toy from her brother, how he felt envious when Lorraine spent even more time alone with Jamie, how it touched him to see Eva feeding her baby brother. Lorraine couldn't believe this was the same Gene who had told her she was silly because she cried when Eva had to be punished. Taking care of the children had awakened Gene's emotions.

Today men are also meeting in groups to talk among themselves about the impact on their lives that has been made by the changes women have brought about. Some men are starting to see what they have missed by concentrating on their jobs and cutting themselves off from the world of children and emotions.

It is difficult for men to face the challenges and demands placed on them by women who want them to be more open about their feelings. Just as women have had to learn the right words to express their emotions and learn a comfortable way of dealing with their feelings, men must go through this process too.

A man may feel vulnerable when he begins to explore his emotions and struggles to find ways to communicate them to others. At this time, he will need your support, guidance, and encouragement. He may want to spend more time talking to you when you have become very busy with your career or your children or your sister's wedding plans. But a husband who wants to learn to share feelings might be a high priority on a wife's list of responsibilities.

CHAPTER 6

Helping Our Children with Their Feelings

CHILDREN HAVE FEELINGS TOO

Dr. David Elkind, a prominent child psychologist, often surprises parents when he lectures to them about their children. Parents, he asserts, share a major misconception about how their children function. They assume that children can *think* like adults, and they become puzzled, impatient, and angry when their children appear less mature than they expect. But when it comes to emotional life, parents often believe that children are immature, that they do not understand feelings and do not experience the range and intensity of emotions of which adults are capable.

In fact, the situation is exactly the opposite. Children are not capable of thinking like adults, and they must go through many stages of development to reach adult levels. But when it comes to feelings, children and adults are not so different after all. Children understand feelings and are quite sensitive emotionally, probably more than most of us realize.

In understanding our children's feelings, we might want to rely on how they act—whether they cry, yell, or look sad or angry—rather than on what they are able to tell us. Young children lack the words to express what they feel, and sometimes even mismatch the words with the feeling. In addition, children are more spontaneous than adults. Although at times children do disguise their feelings, they have not yet learned to hide them as well as adults, and we can rely more on their behavior to understand their emotional lives.

Research shows that newborns appear to experience varying emotional states, which include pleasure, surprise, interest, and disgust. These states are the beginnings of what will eventually become adult emotions. By eight to twelve months, infants show signs of a wide variety of pleasant and unpleasant feelings through smiles, frowns, grimaces, coos, and pouts. These emotions help the infant survive by letting the mother know what he or she needs.

Infants feel content when their basic physical needs are met: when they are fed, dry, cuddled, and comfortable. And they feel frustration that can become terror if it lasts very long when they are hungry, wet, cold, or otherwise physically uncomfortable. Anyone who has been around newborns has noticed that they coo and smile when fed and freshly diapered and when warm and held, and that they howl when hungry, cold, wet, or twisted uncomfortably in their blankets. We might say that our emotional lives begin as reactions to how our bodies feel. As infants mature, their more generalized feelings expand into a range of emotions.

We have already pointed out that adults vary in how emotional they are and in how intensely they experience emotions. Some of these differences in temperament seem to be inborn, and some may be relative to the sex of the infant. Research suggests, for example, that boy infants may be more irritable, cry more, and sleep less than girl infants. They may also respond less to the presence of adults.

Infants' emotions affect their mothers. Crying is not a pleasant sound, and parents usually want to end it. A smiling infant gives the mother more pleasant feelings and lets her feel that she is a better caretaker. In some cases the infant's temperament and the mother's temperament are similar; in other cases they are quite different.

Claudia was a restless and active infant whose mother liked to sit still and always felt content. She had not been prepared for the hard work of dealing with an irritable baby—her first—and became quickly exasperated with Claudia's demands. Sometimes she felt so frustrated that she ran out of the house and left crying Claudia alone for hours at a time.

Soon after birth, infants become very attached to their mothers. This happens as the mother cuddles, feeds, and takes care of the infant's needs. Research has also shown that eye contact between mother and infant seems to be important in establishing an infant's first relationship. This relationship lays the foundation for the infant's capacity to feel emotionally connected to other people throughout his or her life.

The way parents care for their infants seems to affect the emotions the infants can express. Preliminary research by a psychiatrist, Dr. Theodore Gaensbauer, corroborates observations that parents and child psychologists have made about the importance of good caretaking. Dr. Gaensbauer studied abused and neglected infants from families who had not been able to care for them consistently or had abandoned them completely. At twelve to eighteen months of age, these infants were compared to a group of infants who had been better cared for by their parents. The neglected infants showed less pleasure, played less with toys, showed less interest in a stranger, and showed less fear and distress when their mothers left the room. In addition, the neglected infants were consistently more sad than the other group.

This research is important because it is one of the first studies to document the impact of neglectful parents on the emotional capacity of very young children. The neglected infants showed a much smaller range of emotions than the healthier group. They were less sensitive to what went on around them, and their unpleasant emotions, such as anger and sadness, tended to last longer. Dr. Gaensbauer speculates that these children may be particularly vulnerable to depression as adults.

Infants and children are thus more sensitive emotionally than adults often assume. Parents should become careful observers of their children's emotions so they can respond sensitively in both stressful and pleasurable situations. One way parents can do this is to share their own feelings with their children as they become ready, instead of assuming, as we often do, that they are too young to understand.

SHARING EMOTIONS WITH OUR CHILDREN

We can usually begin to tell our children something about what we are feeling once they begin to talk and to match words with certain emotions. When Magda's father died, she and her mother decided that his six-year-old grandson, Paul, was too young to understand what had happened and kept him home from the funeral. But Paul and Grandpa had been very close, so Paul was upset that he would no longer be able to see his great friend, who told "the very best stories." He understood that Grandpa no longer existed in this world, because he had seen him grow sick and old, and he wanted the chance to say good-by to him as everyone else could do at the funeral.

Children are often used to being excluded from adult events such as funerals. But the exclusion left Paul more alone with his grief. His feelings of sadness, loneliness, and anger lasted for a long time.

Death and divorce are two events that parents often hide from children until the very last moment, and then also hide both their own feelings and the ritual called for by an event. Sometimes parents are afraid to tell young children about impending death or divorce or to share their feelings of sadness and fear. In fact, psychologists have found that some parents do not tell their children anything about a divorce until the child wakes up one morning and finds Daddy gone.

Hiding feelings and upsetting events from children fails to provide an outlet for their own emotional reactions. Instead of saying good-by to Grandpa at the funeral and feeling sad along with everyone else for the next several months, six-year-old Paul was left to deal with his sadness and grief all by himself. Because he was not given the chance to express his grief openly, it bothered him longer than it might have had he been included in the family's grieving.

Research on children whose parents are getting a divorce also points up the importance of letting children know what is happening and what to expect—otherwise they are likely to invent fantasies that can be more scary than the actual event. One little girl, never told that her dad would be leaving, became terrified that he had died when she did not find him at home one morning. When her mother finally explained the divorce, Nicole became even more upset, because she worried about what would happen to her father. Psychologist Judith Wallerstein has studied children of divorce extensively and emphasizes the need for parents to let their children in on what is going on and to share feelings of sadness and fright so that the children will understand that it is all right for them to have such feelings too.

It is important for parents to allow children to feel and express a wide range of emotions without thinking that they are bad when they feel angry or sad or hurt. Learning to accept your feelings begins when you are a young child and parents can nurture this process by accepting their children's emotions.

This is not always easy. If we, as adults, have not learned to accept our own unpleasant feelings—envy, hatred, anger, sadness—it will be more difficult for us to allow our children to have these emotions. If we ourselves equate feeling angry with being bad, it is more likely that we will transmit this notion to our children. Awareness and acceptance of our own emotions means that we can better tolerate letting our children express all their emotions.

Sharing feelings with our children does not mean that we can depend on them for emotional comfort or support. Nor can we expect them to share responsibility or help us with the difficult decisions that adults must often make. Although children are capable of experiencing a range of feelings, they handle them on a different level from adults, and can feel frightened and overwhelmed when a parent expects comfort or help in return.

Nicole felt upset and lonely over her father's sudden disappearance, and she became even more frightened when her mother began to cry all the time and talk to her about how lonely and scared she herself felt. Nicole could not handle her own feelings, particularly since she still did not know the story about her father's moving away, and her mother's demands scared her so much that she withdrew to her room and refused to come out for days. This made her mother even more distressed and eventually forced her to talk to a child psychologist about what to do. The situation improved months later, after both mother and daughter received professional counseling.

We noted earlier that while children's emotional capacities may be similar to those of adults, their thinking capacities are different. In fact, the limitations of the way children think affects how they feel. Children often interpret events differently from adults. Adults usually understand cause and effect, so that they do not blame themselves when a parent dies, when a raging storm occurs, or when a dear friend moves far away. But children lack such understanding of how things come to be and often assume that they have caused events to happen through "bad" thinking or "bad" behavior. As a result, they blame themselves for things over which they really had no control.

Elizabeth's grandmother had been in the hospital for a long time before she died. At eight years old, Elizabeth was prevented by hospital rules from visiting her, and this had upset the child greatly. Grandma could barely speak on the phone, so for many weeks Elizabeth neither saw nor talked to her beloved grandmother. As soon as she heard that Grandma had died, she blamed herself, remembering well how she had yelled at Grandma just before she had fallen ill. Elizabeth felt guilty and sad about what she had done, even though her mother explained many times that it was not her fault. It took months for Elizabeth to believe that she had not caused her grandmother's death.

These fears are also common among children whose parents get a divorce. Youngsters often blame their own bad behavior for the separation and have been known to promise to behave better if only their parents will stay together.

This can occur even when they become teenagers. Everyone has noticed, for example, how much teenagers think about themselves and how preoccupied they are with their behavior and appearance. They are constantly afraid of being different from their peers and easily embarrassed and ashamed if they are too different from their friends.

This emotional phase of adolescence may take place because the teenager is developing new thinking capacities. At age eleven or twelve, a child gradually begins to understand that other people think too. Although she realizes this, she still cannot distinguish between what concerns her and what concerns others. She assumes that if she is worried about a pimple on her face, everyone else will focus on that pimple too. The pimple thus becomes emotionally painful out of proportion to its real effect. This at least partially explains why teenagers are so sensitive to criticism and so afraid of standing out from their friends.

Dr. Elkind's analysis of how the development of thinking capacity and emotional life interact helps us understand the stages of our children's development and allows us to be more accepting of what may seem to be peculiar or annoying behavior. It also allows parents to understand the mistakes children and teenagers make in interpreting their emotions as well as those of others.

HELPING CHILDREN WITH THEIR FEELINGS

There are many opportunities for parents to help children deal with emotions. How parents handle and react to children's feelings will affect how the children cope with their emotions as adults. If children have been allowed to feel a range of emotions that have been accepted and understood by parents and not labeled "bad," they are more likely to feel good about themselves as they grow up, and have a better sense of who they are.

None of us are perfect, and most of us have difficulty expressing some emotions. We mentioned earlier, for instance, the special difficulty that women face in accepting and dealing with angry feelings. We often deny anger in ourselves, making it difficult to allow our children, particularly our daughters, to have and express anger.

But it is not just individual parents, or even certain groups of parents, who have difficulty accepting certain feelings and deny them instead. Sometimes whole societies do the same. In American culture, until recently, this was true for feelings of sadness and depression in children. Psychiatrists and psychologists generally believed that children were not capable of feeling depression until they became teenagers. This view was accepted not only by child clinicians but also by a society that wanted to see children as happy and that refused to consider that children might be subject to the same despair experienced by adults.

Very recently, psychologists and psychiatrists have begun to look more closely at young children and at some very early research on infants in orphanages. They have come to see that children too may feel depressed and sad. In fact, such feelings may lie behind part of the behavior problems we observe in some children.

Parents can help their children distinguish among their feelings, and help them know when they feel angry, for example. Most children will feel and express hate toward their parents at some point in time. This is often difficult for parents to accept, but as we discussed in Chapter 2, hate is an inevitable counterpart to love, and we should accept such transient feelings. If we do not accept them, and take our children's hate too personally, responding with anger, we risk making our children feel bad because they have had bad feelings. Over a period of time, such children may feel that a part of them really is bad, and they may begin to like themselves less and feel that they are not worthwhile.

Children seem to have particular trouble distinguishing between being mad and being sad. Adults can make this more difficult by denying that children can feel sad and even depressed. If children are not permitted to feel sad, all that may be left is feeling bad, and they may begin to act that way, getting into trouble with teachers and playmates. In our society, bad children get a lot more attention than sad or depressed children. Parents must work hard to counteract this cultural situation.

Behind a child with behavior problems often lies much sadness. Mrs. Cale, Jason's third-grade teacher, discovered this when she repeatedly had to keep him after school for talking out of turn, refusing to remain in his seat, and generally disrupting the class. She had heard from his second-grade teacher that he had been a model student the year before—curious, attentive, and involved in the classwork—so she could not understand the dramatic change that occurred in late September.

After a few weeks of staying after school with Jason, Mrs. Cale asked gently why he was suddenly having so much trouble and whether he was feeling bad. She found out that over the summer Jason's parents had separated and that Jason missed his father, to whom he was very attached. Mrs. Cale saw how unhappy Jason was about the divorce and discovered that he had been unable to talk to anyone about it because his mother, he reported, cried all the time.

She also found out that Jason believed that he had caused his father to leave, because for weeks before his dad moved out he had refused to pick up his room. Not only did Jason feel bad and guilty about that, but also, now, about his troubling behavior at school. Mrs. Cale realized that Jason's mother felt too overwhelmed to help him with his feelings, so she set up regular visits between Jason and the school psychologist.

It is important to allow our children to experience a range of feeling, but it is also important to let them know that we do not always share those feelings and that we cannot always allow them to act on what they feel. Four-year-old Eddie, for example, was terrified of the dark because "bears would come out of the corner of my room and eat me up." His mother of course did not share this fear, but she knew it was a real one for her son and she did not want to deny his fears. She handled the situation by going into his room each night, acknowledging how scared he felt, turning on the light to search for bears, and showing him that she could not find any and did not think there were any there. This went on for many weeks until one night Eddie told his mother that he thought she was right and the bears had probably gone elsewhere.

It is also important to help children distinguish between having a feeling and acting on it. Eddie's mother did not allow him to leave his bedroom and sleep in hers just because Eddie was scared. Even though five-year-old Stacey was angry that she had not been allowed to stay up late to watch a special television show, her mother did not allow her to act on her anger by throwing things around her room, as she began to do. Both children and adults can get into trouble with other people and with our society's rules. If parents begin early to teach their children the difference between feeling and acting, it is less likely that they will behave badly as they grow up.

But once we deny our children the option of acting on some of their feelings—their anger and envy for example—we must help them learn alternative ways of handling these emotions. We can help them use play to let out their energy and express their feelings, and as they grow older we can help them share their feelings with others instead of acting on them. In some situations, the only available option is helping them accept and regulate their feelings, because there are always times when expressing some feeling is unacceptable even in adults.

Children are keen observers of how adults express their feelings, and what they see can have a great effect on how they express their own feelings as they grow up. But children are also surprisingly adaptable and, if treated well, can recover from emotional upsets in even better shape than before.

AFTERWORD

Despite difficult times in our emotional lives, human beings are remarkably resilient and can bounce back from very upsetting feelings to a stronger and more mature self. We have all noticed, however, that some of us are apt to feel less overwhelmed by our feelings than others, and that when under stress from upsetting events, some people recover more quickly and more easily.

Our emotional resilience depends on many factors. Some we cannot control, others we can learn. We have noted that infants are born with different temperaments, that from the very start some are more irritable and more easily upset than others. And we have discussed the different reactions that mothers have to restless, demanding babies and to smiling babies. What we're born with, taken together with our parents' response to us, affects our capacity to express and regulate our emotions as we grow up. We cannot choose, or control, these formative aspects of our emotional lives, which affect how much we may be overwhelmed by our feelings and how we handle them under stress.

Coping skills, on the other hand, can be learned. While our parents teach us how to express and handle our emotions while we are children, we can add new skills as adults. This is not easy, but it often becomes necessary because of the way our unpleasant emotions may affect others or because of the disruption they may cause. In this way, we may become more resilient emotionally because we choose to struggle with new ways of feeling and of expressing ourselves.

People who are more connected to other human beings—both through close individual relationships and through memberships in groups, such as a church—also appear to be more adaptable emotionally. Relations with others can protect us from stress and from getting overwhelmed by our feelings. They enable us to share feelings and to get help solving emotional problems by talking and by observing how others behave. In close relationships, this kind of help and comfort includes touching and being taken care of. When we feel supported, respected, and cared about by other people, we have more energy to cope with troublesome emotions.

Emotional development continues throughout our lives, and it is important to be aware of the choices we have as adults dealing with our emotions. To change ways of feeling and expressing ourselves may be difficult, and we may find it hard to become connected to people to whom we can give emotionally and from whom we may receive support in return. But the struggle may well be worth it. It can lead to a more pleasurable emotional life, with richer feelings, fewer troublesome disruptions, and the joy of sharing with others.

FURTHER READINGS

Beck, Aaron T. *Cognitive Therapy and the Emotional Disorders*. International Universities Press, 1976.

Benson, Herbert, *The Relaxation Response*. Avon Books, 1976.

Burns, David. *Feeling Good: The New Mood Therapy*. New American Library, 1981.

Elkind, David. *Children and Adolescents*. Oxford University Press, 1974.

Freudenberger, Herbert J., and North, Gail. *Situational Anxiety*. Doubleday & Co., Anchor Books, 1982.

Gilligan, Carol. *In a Different Voice*. Harvard University Press, 1982.

Hammer, Signe. *Daughters and Mothers—Mothers and Daughters*. New American Library, 1975.

House, James S. *Work Stress and Social Support*. Addison-Wesley Publishing Co., 1981.

Kovel, Joel. *A Complete Guide to Therapy: From Psychotherapy to Behavior Modification*. Pantheon Books, 1977.

Lindsey, Karen. *Friends as Family*. Beacon Press, 1982.

Miller, Jean Baker. *Toward a New Psychology of Women*. Beacon Press, 1976.

Mishara, Brian L., and Patterson, Robert D. *Consumer's Handbook of Mental Health*. Signet Books, 1977.

Tavris, Carol. *Anger: The Misunderstood Emotion*. Simon & Schuster, 1982.

3963